Purple Sky Survivalist

Growing Up a Victim of Illusions

Deborah Kinisky

Published by

Blue Sky Thrivalist Co.

Authors Disclaimer:
This is a work of nonfiction and art based on my life and written from my recollections. I have changed the names, descriptions, and identifying characteristics of some individuals to maintain their anonymity. The information contained in this book is not intended to be medical advice or a substitute for the professional medical care. Some of the memories shared are graphic in sexual and violent nature. Reader Discretion is advised.

Copyright © 2016 Deborah Kinisky

Cover by Dianna Bowes
(facebook.com/creativeonthemove/?fref=ts)

Author photo by Bonnie-Jean McAllister
(ealantaphotography.com)

Back Cover Blurb written by Dr. Jodi Abbott (President & CEO NorQuest College Edmonton, Alberta, Canada.

E-book ISBN 978-0-9949271-0-1

Soft Cover ISBN 978-0-9949271-1-8

DEDICATION

I dedicate this book to my blue-eyed angel and little brother Paul, my kind-hearted and strong men-children Dominique and Nathaniel and my sexy and blue sky partner for life Andy.
You are the glue that holds my heart together and your unconditional love, support and understanding has helped me to be a better woman, mom and human being.
Because of you my heart and soul are filled with gratitude.
Thank you.

CONTENTS

Introduction to a Purple Sky

I should have been a tragic statistic who succumbed to severe trauma in my life. Instead I live as an empowered and thriving woman, mother and individual. I am able to do this because I have come to an important understanding about my life, and it all begins with the sky.

Envision a luxuriously warm and ever so slightly breezy summer day. The colors of the landscape that envelops you, varies from vibrant greens to muted olive ones, bright yellows to various browns. You are alone out in the country; the sounds of the city have gotten lost in the pulse of Mother Nature's tranquility.

Imagine lying quietly in the middle of a wheat field; the tall stalks sway hypnotically above as shushing sounds ebb and flow with the wind. Your face and body warm as the sun kisses your skin. Above you are blue skies with nary a wisp of white floating through it. The lullaby of the shushing wheat harmonizes with the buzzing of bees' wings and chirping of crickets as they rub their spiny back legs together. The symphony of nature caresses your ears.

Eyes closed, you reach out and pluck one stalk of wheat and place it in your mouth to gently chew on the tender end. Not a care in the world as you drift off into a sweet, peaceful slumber, content with the simplicity of solid ground below you and a clear blue sky above.

Now I want you to imagine that you've been woken up by a menacing clap of thunder that shakes the earth and startles you back to reality. Your eyes snap open, and you can see that the sky is now a dark and bruised shade of purple as black storm clouds engulf and strangle the blue. Your first thought is to run, but as you look down you realize that you have large chains and shackles attached to your ankles. You realize that you can't escape.

Hail relentlessly pelts your body until you buckle in exhaustion. You are alone, chained, and trapped in this storm where no one can hear your sobs of desperation.

The sky stays purple for so long that you're not sure how much time has passed—days, months, years?—and you start to wonder if such a thing as blue sky ever existed at all. Eventually you stop your sobbing and accept the fact that you will perish under this purple sky.

Now come back to the pages you are holding, and let me thank you for taking that trip with me.

Everyone knows that the sky is blue, right? We know this because as small children we are taught that it's blue by our parents and peers. Instinctively, we believe them its blue, no problem. But what about the child whose parents repeatedly scolds and tells her that the sky isn't blue, that it is in fact purple? The child who grows up with the illusion that it's purple, no matter what a few others outside of her family say. Unlike other children, this child grows up with the delusion that others are wrong, and what they were taught is right. I describe this as *surviving under a purple sky.*

The heart inside of me knew that the sky was supposed to be blue, that blue was normal, but my head was trained to focus on believing in the purple. At times, I thought I saw shades of blue in the distance, but it would quickly disappear, or I couldn't quite get to it.

I'm a firm believer that there are times when all the pieces of the puzzle at long last just click into place—our *aha* moments. We've all had them; unfortunately, mine didn't come and change my sky to blue until I was almost forty years of age. But they happened, and they can happen to you too. That's the important part: the possibility.

These epiphanies helped me finally realize I was no longer a victim of the traumas that I endured throughout my life. They showed me I was strong, nurturing, and thriving because of that endurance. I decided and I chose not to be a sad statistic. Being newly aware of myself led me to a new series of events. It allowed me to finally live victoriously and love voraciously. These events include graduating from college at forty-two, finding true love, and becoming an author and successful entrepreneur shortly after.

I am here because of one simple thing: LOVE.

In my opinion love is the most healing power in the world and glimpses of it are what kept me alive and helped me to unlearn that a purple sky was normal. I believe that if a person knows they are loved and cherished, they can achieve anything that she sets her mind to and beyond.

In my first book, *HerStory ~ Victim to Victorious,* I ripped the proverbial Band-Aid off decades-old wounds and exposed the raw and violent truth of the secrets and hurts of my life. It was a tear-, snot-, and anxiety-soaked experience, because I'd never condensed my deepest, darkest secrets together or written a book exposing them before. Other than a handful of loving and supportive family and friends who cheered me on, I experienced and wrote it alone. It was a purging and personal therapy that was long overdue and necessary to happen in order for me to completely heal. I shared my story because I was worth it, just like you and your story are worth it.

The whole experience cleansed me more deeply than I thought I needed to be. I willingly allowed eyes from around the world to read my anguished words and hoped that I wouldn't be judged harshly. I'm not an actress, a television personality or known musician. I'm just one regular, ordinary woman you pass each day on the street. You might not even notice I'm there. Would readers find me worthy of their time or attention?

The response I received was overwhelming and unanimous, and I was showered with the essential ingredients to life: love, support, and encouragement. I learned that while living under a clear blue sky I wasn't alone in having a horrific past.

I chose to take on writing my life into a series of books because I wanted to express less of the hurt while showcasing more of the healing aspect of my story. My intention is that my words will be used as a tool for others to find their hidden qualities and utilize them.

Every letter forming each word further lightened the darkness that pent up, traumatic secrets had burned onto my soul and dispersed that darkness out into the universe. I discovered that I wasn't alone on my journey of self-care. I was surrounded by women from my past, present, and future who confirmed that I was the voice of every woman who isn't strong enough yet to raise her own in protest. I mattered.

The biggest difference is my own full readiness to step outside of my story and into my strength and clarity of purpose. Through sharing the heart of my story, I'm here to help you find your own voice.

My hope is to encourage anyone who lives under a bruised and purple sky to come forward and reclaim a blue sky life. You are worth it; you matter and you are never alone. My request, my invitation is this: please realize your true potential in life.

The time has come for all of us to break the silence and allow ourselves to speak the unspeakable and tell the untold. This doesn't have to be in the form of a confessional book like I have done but in your own way to release the darkness that's been carefully hidden inside.

This I know: if I can thrive, so can you.

Deborah

Two Little Worms in a Bucket of Mud

I was born in Maple Ridge, British Columbia, on January 28, 1968. Maple Ridge was the first of numerous residences where I'd live over the coming years. I was a healthy, bouncing baby girl with all of my fingers and toes and the newest addition to the family of a mother, father, and three-year-old brother. It was on that day that my life officially started, and the very same day I believe that the nurturing ended. Or perhaps it never began at all.

I was an accident after all. I learned over the years that having children was not at the top of my mother's priority list when she got pregnant with my brother or me, yet the act of making babies by mistake was at an all-time high. Much later, my mother told me that my brother and I were the only two children out of six pregnancies that actually came to term.

At the time of my birth, my father was running with the Grim Reapers Motorcycle Club. He was in and out of jail for a better part of my earlier years. I had even less of a relationship with him as a small child than I did with my mother. He was around, though, because he had us living a highly transient lifestyle as he outran the law. We moved fifteen times by the time I was eighteen. I also know he was around when I was small because my mother would threaten me with him as a punishment when I became an annoyance to her.

With her face red and pinched with anger, she'd point in the direction of my room. She kept her voice low and menacing and each syllable was punctuated as she'd say: "Get to your room *now!* Your dad will be in to deal with you when he gets home."

The thought of this frightened me. I didn't want to be *dealt with*. I'd scurry to my room, hide under my blanket, and cry while I waited in fear of the unknown. Her threats were hollow though. By the time he'd get home, I'd already cried myself to sleep and was no longer an annoyance.

My brother, Ryan was three years older than me and in the beginning was a loving, sweet older brother. When I look at pictures of us from that time, I can see the joy and innocence in the smiles on our cherub faces. He was a beautiful, exuberant little boy, and I was his adored baby sister. In our earlier years he was at times my only friend, my closest ally, and my fearless protector.

My first lucid memory of this protection came to me as a recurring dream that haunted me frequently as I was growing up. I was three years old and he was six. We were alone in a kitchen that had a large window making the room bright. I was standing on a stepstool at an island in the middle of the room, facing the back door of the house.

Ryan was on the opposite side of the island from me with his back was to the door. He was struggling with a can opener to open a can of fruit cocktail far enough so that we could scoop some out, but his attempts weren't going well. He continued to pry the can open; the determination evident on his face.

I was intent on watching his every move and grinning from ear to ear in anticipation. I knew that if he could get it open, we would eat something. We were both so focused on the task at hand that we were oblivious to what was going on around us.

I heard the *snick* and *ting* of tin-leaving-tin. Success! At the same instant there was a loud crashing noise that distracted me from looking at the partially open can. I jerked my head up and looked towards the back door where the noise had come from. I saw that it was being knocked off the hinges by men dressed in black who were carrying guns. As the nightmare ended I'd bolt upright out of bed. I was ripped from sleep and lying in a pool of cold sweat with an accelerated heart rate and a face soaked with tears.

The reality of that day is that Ryan and I were taken into foster care by British Columbia's provincial government for protection from the neglect of my parents. The men kicking in the door were doing a drug bust on our house and found two children left alone by the babysitter. Somehow, my parents were later allowed to take us back home only to fend for ourselves again. My father was in jail, my mother returned from partying with her friends across the border, and we all returned to our purple-hued skies.

My mother is a small but powerful woman who stands around 5'2". For most of my childhood she was quite abundant in girth. She had large, natural breasts that were left unrestrained to sag disturbingly under the colorful muumuus she would wear. More times than not her fine, sandy blonde hair, usually worn at ear length, was permed to the perfect frizz. Like a mood ring, her eyes changed from blue to green to black with how she felt and her levels of intoxication.

In 1973 when I was five-years old and Ryan was eight, we moved to residence number three: a house with a big front yard in Abbotsford, BC. My brother and I shared a large bedroom upstairs but had separate beds. At that point in our lives, he and I were still very young and not yet too tainted by the family we had been born into; thus, we had a playful, innocent relationship.

Based on my recollections from this age, it's apparent that being spanked by our mother was not a new thing for either of us. We'd both been hit by her before, and it wasn't uncommon for us to get smacked repeatedly, with or without various implements. It all depended on where we were in the house and what was within our mother's reach. If she couldn't get to something fast enough, she would just smack us with her hands and at other times with wooden spoons or belts. Given her actions, it would seem that we were an aggravation for her at every turn.

I could mince words here, but I won't because what she inflicted on my brother and I would not be classified as a spanking in any sense of the word. She beat us. Her beatings were always accompanied with a verbal barrage of insults.

She spewed hate with ever word. "You're bad, fucking bad! I should have aborted you! No one wanted you, wants you, or will ever want you! Shut up, shut up, *shut up!*"

She'd repeat these atrocities numerous times throughout my life.

One beating in particular stands out above all the rest. It would've been a normal afternoon that we were left to entertain ourselves, which wasn't an unusual situation in our house. Our mother was either in bed taking a nap while high on morphine, watching her soap operas, or just wasn't there at all because she was taking what I would later call her "mini vacation," which meant she was in the psychiatric ward or mental hospital.

We were in our bedroom and were goofing around on my bed, rolling around, having a pillow fight, tickling, laughing, and being silly children. To entertain me, Ryan was rolling himself off the side of the bed pretending he was fainting onto the floor and would make an *ooof* sound, as he'd grab his knee or tummy.

His antics were funny to me, and I'd start giggling, quietly at first. He repeated it over and over again making each time more dramatic than the last, making me laugh even harder and louder. We'd let out excited squeals of laughter in spite of the fact our mother was trying to take a nap downstairs. We knew this because she'd yelled from her bedroom a few times already telling us to keep the noise level down. When she yelled, we instantly stopped what we were doing and listened intently for sounds of movement below us; we'd been in this situation before.

After a few minutes of silence from downstairs and with us being children, boredom took over and within minutes the hush was broken again by stifled giggles. These turned into laughter, which ultimately lead to more yelling from our mother.

Her yelling turned into screaming. "You are fucking bad kids, and if you can't shut the fuck up I'll teach you a lesson!"

Then we heard her start to move downstairs, open a drawer and then close it. Ryan and I looked at each other. We knew this was not going to be good. We knew we were safe in the yelling stage, but we'd made the mistake of letting it surpass that. We'd elevated her anger to the moving stage, and we both knew what that meant: it was time to get a lickin'.

We heard her thumping loudly up the stairs, and judging by the aggression in her stomps, we knew that we were in for some trouble. She burst through the doorway with a look of hatred on her face, power in her stance, and a new implement in her hand.

This form of punishment we'd never seen before. The unfamiliar strap was a three-foot long, quarter-inch wide section of conveyor belt. As she moved toward the bed, my brother and I quickly scrambled against the wall. I saw fear on his face as we looked to each other for courage.

We both tried frantically to get under the thin blanket on my bed. Ryan's body curled around mine like a ball, protecting me from what we both knew was about to come. We knew from experience that if we could get under the blanket it wouldn't hurt as badly when she repeatedly hit us until her anger was expended.

We lay there, our tiny bodies intertwined like two little worms in a bucket of mud, squirming under the thin blanket trying to evade her strikes. With every lash, in a panicked rush of whisper, we told her we were sorry for being loud, repeating that we would be a good. We would be quiet.

We learned fast to apologize quickly and profusely and then just take the pain, not yell out, and stay as still as we could. She ran out of steam soon enough and left like nothing had happened, leaving my brother and I alone to sob ourselves to sleep, hoping to wake up to a better day. We always did, and just the fact that we had made it through another bout of our mother's rage was blue sky enough for me.

Some days I'd play outside in the yard and entertain myself with bugs and other creepy crawlies of all shapes and sizes hiding in the dirt. I'd escape into their tiny world and explore. I'd chase them down or catch them because I didn't mind getting up close and personal with insects—except for spiders, which I observe from more of a distance.

Most days, however, were spent in the isolation of my bedroom with the creativity of my imagination as my only toy, but there were insects there too. I'd sit on my bed with a shoebox resting ever so lovingly on my lap. Nestled in the bottom of the shoebox was a layer of paper towel, and on that paper towel was a quiet activity that could entertain me for hours when I had no humans around: my flea collection. They were so tiny but seemed so strong, and could jump so far. I was fascinated by them and too young to know that they were not a good thing to have around.

I'd find them jumping around in the blanket on my bed. I'd catch them and gently place them into the shoebox, one at a time. I'd quickly close the lid so they couldn't escape. I'd take them out of the box one or two at a time, examine their tiny bodies, and have a pretend little flea circus. I'd place them on my fingertip and watch as they'd jump back into the box. Sometimes I'd put them on different parts of my hand, the outside of my leg, or pretend race them in the box where I could see them better against the white of the paper towel. Most times, however, they flung themselves further than I expected, and ended up lost in the tumble of my bed again. This didn't bother me because I could simply look through my blankets and find another one.

It makes a person wonder what kind of child was so desperate for activity and companionship that they played with fleas. My heart breaks whenever I think of this because that kind of child was me. I didn't have toys to play with or know what a friend was yet and learned how to entertain myself early on. I was comfortable with my isolation because there was no pain or hurt when I was alone. Pain and hurt were all I knew under an already darkening sky.

In my early years, my love and appreciation had extended to larger living things like plants and animals, domestic and wild. We had a red-tailed hawk named Rahja for a few months that watched me with amber eyes as closely as I watched her. One of her wings was broken and healing and my father had been asked to teach her how to fly again so she could be released back into the wild.

While training her he would wear two thick, leather gloves on the hand that she rested on so that her razor sharp talons wouldn't pierce his skin. To calm her he would slip a small leather hood, much like a bonnet, over her head and tie it under her chin. To restrain her he would loop a simple tether to her leg. I was always eager to help him with the training and use of these intricate tools whenever he let me.

I'd examine her closer and gently stroke her silky feathers and wings to soothe her. I wondered how they worked and what it felt like to fly. I'd felt feathers before but never on a living, breathing predator. Though I'd been part of her rehabilitation and was happy to see her healthy enough to leave, I was also sad to see her go. This was also about the time that I found my nurturing nature had begun to bloom.

Liquid Brown Gaze and Mean Brown Eyes

We were living at a camp where my father was working in Rainbow Lake, Alberta: population 583. This was our fourth move in six years. My father would take us to the Rainbow Lake garbage dump, not to drop garbage off like other folks, but to go "treasure diving" through those other folks' trash to see what we could salvage for our own family's use. We would rip open the bags and pick out bottles, car parts, clothes, or anything that my family could use or my father could sell.

On one of our treasure hunts, my mother kicked a bag open that contained the carcass of a dead foal that was covered in maggots, and the disgusting smell sickened me. Trying to stay as far away from the stench as possible, I aimlessly rifled through bags as I moved stuff around and quit paying attention to where I was going. Unknowingly, I'd made my way to the ridge at the top of the garbage heap. I tripped over something and stumbled a bit, bringing my mind back from daydreaming to where I actually was.

I scrutinized my hands to see if I'd gotten anything gross on them, and when I looked up again, two hundred feet in front of me sat a large brown bear, with her cub peeking out from behind her.

As I locked eyes with the mother bear and her liquid brown gaze, my body froze instantly. I was shocked but unexpectedly calm. We stared at each other for about fifteen seconds, and then she looked away from me. I'd read about bears and knew she was dangerous, but I felt no fear, only admiration, as I watched her shield her cub from potential danger. I was mesmerized by her maternal and protective energy, which was such a contrast from what I had received. There was no one protecting me.

Ever so slowly, I inched my way backwards over the ridge, never taking my eyes off of the mother bear that thankfully did not pay me any more attention as she walked in the other direction, with her cub in tow.

When I felt a safe enough distance away I turned and ran as fast as I could to my parents, still near the bottom of the heap. Excitedly I told my dad what happened with the bear.

His response was, "I wish I had my gun," which prompted me to walk away so that I could treasure my memory before it became more tainted by his words.

A few weeks later, I had a second encounter with a bear, and it was even more up close and personal. It was a quiet, sunny afternoon, and I was a sitting on the front steps of our trailer watching the clouds roll by when the silence was abruptly disturbed by some men whistling and yelling. This piqued my curiosity, and I walked towards the excited voices. When I got to where the commotion was coming from, there was a frenzy of activity, and I wanted to see what was in the middle of it. As I got closer by ducking between legs and shifting the men's bodies with my tiny frame, I saw it.

It was a bear cub. I was mesmerized by it, drawn to it, and I wanted to touch it. The man who was holding it had to muzzle its snout because it was crying so very loudly for its mother, who I soon discovered, was being held against her will in the shed that held the work trucks.

While the baby bear was bleating, its mother was trying to rock the walls of the garage off and was doing a pretty good job. I secretly wished that someday someone would want to rock the walls off to save me, but that time wasn't now. Inside, I was that bleating cub but my cries were caused by a mother who was supposed to be protecting me, unlike this cub's mother.

Eventually everyone around us got to see and pet the baby, and then it was my turn. In what seemed like slow motion but only lasted a second, I stared into the baby bear's dark, amber eyes and could sense the fear it was feeling as I quickly and gently stroked its dense quivering fur before they let it go. It shot like a rocket into the bush and scurried to the top of a tree. Some brave or stupid soul got up on the roof the shed out of harm's way, then leaned down to open the door. One very pissed off mother bear was released and went barreling out like a bat out of hell to tend to her distressed offspring.

In 1975 when I was seven years old, we moved to residence number five, which was a farm in Onoway, Alberta: population 485. I was in full out tomboy/farm girl mode as I loved being free to explore life in all of its forms and being outdoors where I could escape the insanity and isolation that was already my life. I had developed a special fondness for farm animals because more times than not I preferred the company of a four-legged creature over two-legged ones. Where we lived, animals were always more readily available than people, and that worked for me. I can never recall a time in my life when I've been without a pet. Even though we lived a transient lifestyle, moving from small town to small town, there were always animals around.

Mostly we lived out in the middle of nowhere. On our farm we had domestic, farm, and exotic animals, from cows, horses, and pigs to chickens, turkeys, ducks, and—my favorite of all—goats. It may have been the animals in my life that kept me either safe or sane and in many cases both.

On one particular afternoon I was in the loft of the barn sitting on the straw and playing with a kitten. I looked up and saw a few trucks rolling down the dusty, gravel driveway into our yard. We didn't get any company, so I was curious who was coming. I climbed down from the loft and made my way to the door so that I could peek out. I couldn't see what was in the trucks, but I sure could hear what was in the crates.

I went from peeking to a full on run towards them. In those crates were dogs, dogs, and more barking and baying dogs! I'd never heard so many dogs in my whole life and I was ecstatic when I watched an endless line of them exit the back of the trucks. As it had turned out, my father had agreed to board several men's coyote-hunting dogs, which ended up being fifty-six of the most beautiful creatures on four paws. Yes—fifty-six!

There were greyhounds, borzois, whippets, Irish wolfhounds, huskies, and Irish setters of every shape, size, and color, and I wanted to cuddle each and every one of them. Over the course of their stay with us I'm sure I did just that. Some more than others. My favorite was a small, horse-sized, shaggy-haired Irish wolfhound aptly named Blue because his fur was an extraordinary grayish-blue color.

He was timid and shy like me, and the other dogs weren't very nice to him, but when I greeted him he would wag and whip his wiry tail so hard that his whole big body shook, right down to his wet, pointy nose. His uncontrollable shaking made me giggle every time, so I greeted him back enthusiastically every time.

About a week after their arrival the dominant dogs attacked and ripped Blue's neck open, requiring surgical repair. My father rushed him into the house and placed him on the table where I soothed his bloody head as my father stitched up his gaping neck. No anesthetic, just the shushing of my voice in his ear and the steady caressing of his blood-matted fur.

I didn't leave his side for those first couple of days and even slept in the barn with him to make sure he was alright. Under my tender loving care, it wasn't long before he was up and running and being accepted more by the other dogs although he preferred to be with me. Summer turned into fall and the dogs' owners needed them to go back to work hunting coyotes and as quickly as they'd arrived it seemed they were gone. I couldn't bear to watch them get packed up, so I sat in the barn loft straw snuggling and using a kitten as a tissue.

Later I watched the dust kicked up by the trucks rolling down the gravel driveway, sad that they were going in the wrong direction. Those departing trucks were filled with valuable lessons of friendship and loyalty in its truest and simplest form. A dog, appropriately named Blue, and all of his friends had given me a glimpse of love. And after he was gone I was alone again.

My parents would often go to auctions in the area to purchase large quantities of products that were needed on the farm, like dog food, cases of cereal, and powdered milk. Because of those random purchases, Ryan and I ate Grape-Nuts and Corn Flakes cereal every morning, noon, and night for years. He liked the Corn Flakes and would put so much sugar on them that they'd almost melt into his bowl like an orange, puddle of syrupy goop that always grossed me out.

I, however, preferred the Grape-Nuts because in my eyes eating pellets of what tasted like compressed sawdust swelled up by some watered-down powdered milk was just more appetizing. Besides that, I couldn't get over the smell of the concoction that appeared to bubble in my brother's bowl like a science experiment.

They could buy anything at the auctions from a vehicle to livestock to dry and household goods. My parents would often take me with them, and I loved it because I was a free-spirited and independent child who was given freedom to roam through all of the animal pens as my parents were off bidding on livestock or supplies. I'd spent a better part of my short life being self-sufficient as my parents lived their lives, and I somehow maneuvered through mine. I was comfortable being on my own already. I preferred it, actually, and would fearlessly jump up on the sides of the fencing containing the colts, calves, and—my favorites—the baby goats and piglets, so that I could pet or coo at them.

One afternoon I went to the auction with just my father. I roamed and inspected the livestock area immediately. I was standing on a railing looking down at a momma pig feeding her babies when a man I didn't know approached the side of the pen. I didn't speak to or acknowledge him as I continued to watch the babies and minded my own business.

He said, "I have cuter piglets that I'll let you play with. Your parents told me they will buy you one after you come pick it out."

Not knowing any better, I followed him. I was excited as he led me to the back of the arena where he said his piglets were. I couldn't wait to hold them, play with them, and pick one.

When I arrived at the enclosure I tried to get up on the railing for a better view but this railing was a bit higher, and I couldn't quite get up. As I lifted my leg up high the man swiftly placed his hand full on in my crotch. I instantly tensed, gasped, and squirmed desperately as I tried to remove my body from his grasp while he pretended to help hoist me up. I was silent but looked frantically at his face as he squeezed my arm tightly and ground his hand deeper into me. Darkness clouded my vision as I stopped struggling, and he quickly released his grip and placed me on the ground.

I finally exhaled and ran away as fast as my oxygen-deprived, little lungs and legs could muster in search of my dad. I was scared, confused, and crying loudly for him as I ran around the arena, just as the bear cub had run up the tree when released. I was now that cub in distress, and I needed protection. Where was my mother bear?

When I found him I ran into his arms and sobbed into his shoulder. As I told him what'd happened, his face got red and screwed tightly into an angry grimace. Some people had gathered nearby and listened as I described the man whose image I'd always hold in my mind's eye. My father abruptly set me aside and told me to wait while they all ran outside of the building looking for this man. Someone yelled that they'd called the police, and the next thing I knew I was being scooped back up into my dad's arms.

He quickly placed me in the truck and said, "He got away and we have to go." We high-tailed it out of there back to the farm and my solitude.

And that was it. No one ever spoke about it after that. Other than my dad's abrupt initial reaction at the auction, the fact that I'd been sexually assaulted seemed to have been unnoticed and forgotten.

I, however, didn't forget. I was reminded at night when I closed my eyes and saw the man's mean, brown eyes staring into mine. I was taught that violations and being hurt didn't matter. That I didn't matter. My family of animals thought I mattered, which most days was more than enough. I was surviving and continued to use the affection of critters to offer me glimpses of love. I preferred it that way, though. I'd never been hurt intentionally or ridiculed by anything with four legs, feathers, or fur

You Are My Sunshine

In 1976 I turned eight years old. We relocated two times in that year; moves number six and seven. The first place we lived was a two-story, brown condo complex in Peace River, Alberta. We had just moved from the farm in Onoway where my closest friends all had four legs. We were now living in a town that had neighbors within walking distance, and those neighbors had children both me and my brother's age. Ryan's new friendships kept him occupied, which I didn't mind because I was occupied too.

We'd moved so frequently and always lived in rural locations, so making friends never came easy for either of us. My mother strictly enforced silence, which molded us both to be highly introverted. This new living situation was foreign to us children. We weren't used to such close proximity to other people. Living in a setting that had girl children my age and a swing set in the complex was like a dream come true to me—a neglected, abused little girl. It offered me a fun place to run and play and the promise of something I'd never experienced before: friendship on two legs.

For the first time in my life I had a girlfriend, and her name was Carrie. She was a blonde-haired, blue-eyed little girl who was my age and wore dresses like a girl. Not her brother's hand-me-downs. She was pretty, spoiled rotten, and loud. She had a lot of dolls and toys to play with, was funny, always laughing, and loved to sing—loudly. This little girl was instrumental in helping me start to heal as a broken child.

I remember the last day I spent with her because it was the first time in my life that I was able to express myself without repercussions; she taught me to sing...*loud!*

One afternoon not too long after we moved into the complex, my brother went out into a nearby wooded area with a friend of his. They both sported .22 rifles to hunt for squirrels or gophers. Unfortunately, the only thing that got shot that day other than a few trees was my brother. I can still picture him quickly limping towards the condo supported by his friend, with blood all over his foot.

As he approached my mother, who was in hysterics after seeing the blood, he told us they had heard a noise and thought it was a bear. It spooked them and his friend flinched and accidentally shot him in the foot point blank. The bullet of the .22 pushed the metal eyelet of his running shoe straight through making a clear hole and exiting into the ground. They brought home the eyelet and bullet to prove the story. My parents needed to take him to the hospital and left me in the care of Carrie's parents. I was worried about my brother, but I was happy to be spending some time with my new friend and her pretty dolls.

Carrie and her brother had tons of toys in their rooms. More than any one child would ever want or need and I was thrilled to be able to play with them. After a while of playing, she said she wanted to go outside, but I didn't want to go. I was quite content to sit in the midst of dolls and more dolls. She roughly grabbed the one that I was playing with by the arm and strolled outside into the courtyard of our complex. Like a horse to a carrot, I followed the doll and Carrie outside.

She wanted to go to the swing set, which had one swing and an attached teeter-totter. Despite my initial reluctance we played on that contraption for what seemed like hours. Each of us stood on an end of the teeter-totter and pumped our little legs joyfully. It arched up as high as it could go before the leg posts would pop loose from the ground and almost dump us off.

When I first heard Carrie begin to sing I thought she was crazy and needed to quiet down. I shushed her. I didn't want her to get into trouble. My eyes darted around apprehensively to see who was going to come punish her for being so noisy and disruptive. But no one came. She repeatedly sang the same song over and over. She smiled and encouraged me to sing with her, but I was happy enough having the wind blow through my dandelion-puff, blonde hair, and the sun on my face with a new girlfriend. The sky looked almost blue to me.

After her incessant prompting I too began to sing, quietly at first. Then realizing that no one was there to silence me, I began to sing with her—and loudly. In a happy place in my mind, I can still envision us with our hands gripping the pole in the middle as we braced for a fall. The courtyard echoed with our raucous childlike laughter and *"You Are My Sunshine"* being sung at the top of our lungs. I learned that day that it was okay to make noise, have fun, and be a child. I relished every second of that lesson.

My parents' return with my brother and Carrie needing to go home for dinner brought our vocal session to a halt. In her hurry to get home, Carrie left her doll on the ground. Despite the fun of our afternoon, I felt angry that she held such little respect for this baby doll, and I decided to steal it for myself.

It was just a silly doll to her, but to me it was so much more than that. I knew firsthand how it felt to be cast aside and neglected. I couldn't stand idle and watch things being mistreated—inanimate or not—and wanted to teach her a lesson. She would never miss it anyhow because she had so many other dolls, and since I didn't have toys of my own, I planned on having much fun with the unwanted doll. It would be my new girlfriend and would sleep with me at night like a real baby, which is exactly what I named her: Baby. That night I lay in bed snuggled closely to Baby and drifted off to sleep. I was happy and dreamed of blue skies, laughter, and singing.

Around 5:30 a.m. the next morning, just before the sun was coming up, the neighborhood was woken up by a woman screaming for help outside in the courtyard. As I ran out of the door with my family, I could see smoke billowing out the front door of Carrie's family's condo.

Her mother stood in front of their house crying and screaming, *"No! No! No!* Carrie is still inside!"

When I looked up at her bedroom window, I could see her. She was trapped upstairs by the flames on the staircase, and no one had realized it until it was too late. While we waited for the fire department, one of the neighbors brought a ladder to the front of the building and tried climbing to her bedroom window several times without success. Even my mother tried a few times to climb up the side of the condo to break the window, but the roof was too hot for her or anyone else to get onto.

So many people yelled and pleaded with Carrie to come to the window.

Break the window! Someone break the window!

They were trying to protect her but couldn't. All she had to do was throw something at it, and the glass would have shattered. I can close my eyes and still see her standing there with an expression of complete terror on her face, crying...and then she was just gone.

The days following her passing were somber and quiet as everyone spoke in hushed tones around me. I'd never experienced human death before and wasn't sure how to act or react. My mother was crying inconsolably in her room, so I figured it was alright for me to do the same. I spent my time in my preferential solitude where I mourned more than the loss of a friend. I mourned that no one was able to protect me or her from harm.

Carrie seemed to matter though; everyone had tried to help her and cared that she'd been killed, yet I was still here and didn't matter. I cried in my room while cuddling and soaking Carrie's Baby with my snot and tears. I'd sit on the swing or teeter-totter while tears of grief streamed down my face while quietly singing "You Are My Sunshine."

This was further validation that I wasn't worth protecting.

Her mother told us that Carrie had gone into the closet and *asphyxiated*. I didn't know what that word meant, but I silently wondered if it was my punishment for stealing her doll. I kept Baby with me and treasured her for many years.

Shortly after the fire, we moved for the second time that year. It was fall, and the temperature was dropping. As we drove up a winding dirt road into the forest in the middle of nowhere, my dad exclaimed, "This is where we're going to live."

I thought he was joking. He wasn't.

When we first arrived at the property, there was nothing but trees for days on a piece of land just outside of Peace River, Alberta. We worked day and night with axes and chainsaws to clear full-sized trees and saplings for enough room to build a basic house. We survived there for eight months with four walls and a roof but no plumbing or electricity.

Thankfully we were able to burn all of the tree wood in the stove to keep us warm. A short time after the structure was erected the first snow fell and the season progressed as a typical Alberta winter does: rapidly. In my opinion it was almost like we were living in a barn, because our goats Romeo and Julius would sleep in the house with us like dogs. They were better than dogs because they gnawed the new tree shoots that were growing back around the house, something a dog cannot do.

One time my mother placed a two-liter bottle of orange soda pop to one of the goats' lips. It gripped the bottle with its front teeth and tipped it up, suckling on it like a baby with a teat. When he was done and the bottle fell away, the goat had a bright orange moustache. I'd never seen anything so funny, and my mother and I howled with laughter together.

Laughter shared with my mother was unexpected and rare because she wasn't mentally or physically present for the most part. When she was around she would bark orders at me, belittle me, or shoo me out of her way. Even at that young age I was so desperate for love, affection, and glimpses of blue sky that I had to hold onto whatever thread of happiness I could find. They were few and far between.

On the night of December 24, 1976, when I was eight years old and my brother was eleven, my father drove my mother into Edmonton. She was in need of a mini vacation from reality at the local psych ward, which left my brother and me alone in a rickety, half-built shack in backwoods Alberta on Christmas Eve. My parents were still not back on Christmas day, and we had no food in the house. My brother and I decided to take matters into our own hands, so he grabbed his .22 rifle. I equipped myself with my pellet gun, and we trekked into the forest in knee-deep snow to find something to eat.

We saw a few grouse and a rabbit, but they moved too quickly for our small bodies to catch them in the deep snow. I looked up into a tree and saw a squirrel poke out its head to see what was going on. I pointed at it for my brother to see. It turned out he was a pretty good shot; the squirrel fell dead onto the ground. We took it back to the house where we skinned it and cleaned it like we had seen our father do before to so many animals—usually much bigger.

That night we feasted on freshly diced squirrel meat cooked over the wood-burning stove, with some water and flour added to make gravy. That was the only present we received that year: a warm meal in our bellies to keep us snug through the night and one to this day that I'm thankful for.

Ryan and I had survivalist minds and headstrong yet quiet personalities that developed early because of our lack of parental nurturing and guidance. We had each other, our four-legged friends, and knew self-sufficiency was the only option. I mimicked what he and my father were doing to supply us with food, and I paid close attention to the life cycles that were around me. I learned quickly how to be resourceful out of necessity and how to survive in tough circumstances.

Once the snow melted in spring it was time to move again. My father either realized it wasn't easy trying to raise a family without electricity or running water or the law caught up to us. All I knew was that without discussion my four-legged friends went missing, and we were told to pack up our few tattered belongings

Pink Lemonade and Vodka and Sex 101

In 1977 I turned nine years old, and our family encountered our eighth move in nine years. This time it was to Berwyn, Alberta: population 463. It was a short drive as we moved at night under the cover of darkness from our ill-equipped, ramshackle house into a single wide trailer. Ryan and I shared a small bedroom with a tiny window and bunk beds. It was a semi-rural neighborhood that offered a lot of space behind our trailer, and we had neighbors within walking distance.

I was given no time to adjust to my new surroundings and was taken to school and enrolled the first morning. To provide me with breakfast and a lunch for school my parents stopped at the grocery store and bought me a box of twelve cinnamon-flavored granola bars and a large bunch of bananas. The other kids were nice to me that day because I shared my food with them, and I felt that I was genuinely liked.

The next day I returned with a normal lunch and school went back to being a social struggle for me. I wore my brother's hand-me-down clothes, most of which were dirty, scuffed, and weathered, and the kids teased me, saying that I was poor, and that I smelled of pee.

I didn't have many friends and spent most of my time as a loner because being alone was far less painful than being reminded of my shortcomings. It was about that time when I became enslaved to a purple sky as twisted lessons about sexuality were deeply ingrained into my vulnerable and already misguided understanding. I again learned that I was unlovable and to expect nothing because I was insignificant, and I didn't matter. I watched and learned as my parents became more social and were—dare I say it—waist deep in the swinger scene. They frequently had parties with different friends. Some I knew, most I did not.

My parent's new friends would sometimes bring their children to our house, and we would all hang out together while the adults mingled separately. One young girl I met talked loudly and incessantly until I held a pillow over her face to momentarily silence her. She avoided me after that even though I was only trying to teach her a valuable lesson that I'd learned: best to keep quiet.

One night my parents had a party with some people we were unfamiliar with and they sent my brother and me to bed early. The music and people outside our bedroom door were enticing, and my brother and I became restless. How could we sleep when there was music, laughter, and snacks going on out there? Why didn't we get to have parties?

Ryan and I snuck out separately to check what all the noise was about and to listen to the music. Our mother would soon discover us in our hiding place and scowl at us for interrupting her fun. She angrily ushered us back into our room. She warned us about coming back out as she slammed our bedroom door and went back to the party at hand. This didn't deter us and we continued to be drawn by the music.

During one of my turns to sneak out, I saw my mother and father oddly wrapped around people that I didn't know. They were kissing and touching each other in the same place where the man at the auction had touched me. I was confused because I couldn't understand how they could be enjoying something that hurt so much. I must've made a noise because my mother noticed me peeking around the corner, yet again interrupting her.

In her intoxication or desire to remove us from the equation, she grabbed two tall glasses and filled them with punch—her favorite mix of pink lemonade and vodka—then sent us back to our room to drink it. That was my first taste of alcohol, the sweet nectar that it was. We drank half the glass and began laughing at nothing and everything and didn't have a care in the world. Near the bottom of the glass it was no longer funny to me, and the room began to spin, so I closed my eyes to sleep and the party went on without me.

Shortly after my first drink I had my second and third, and then I stopped counting. I started smoking cigarettes. It seemed like the right thing to do; both my parents smoked, and my brother was also smoking already.

I wanted to be cool like him, so I watched, and I learned like I had in the past.

Shortly after my 10th birthday my brother introduced me to smoking marijuana for the first time.

"I have a present for you." He led me to the kitchen and opened the freezer door. He reached into the back and pulled out a rolled up plastic bag with dried leaves in it. He told me that our father had grown what was in the bag and had stashed it in the freezer so that no crazy person could lace it with kitchen chemicals. He took some out and explained that it was like smoking cigarettes but would make me laugh, and I wanted nothing more in life than to laugh. So he rolled it, and we smoked it, and I loved how it made me feel happy inside where darkness normally resided.

It was shortly time later that my brother pushed me out of his life both figuratively and literally. He mimicked the insults I had endured from our mother for years, which confirmed they must be true, if he was saying them too. If his verbal tactics didn't work to get me to leave, he'd shove me or put a fist in my face to get his point across.

By that age I knew I was a mistake, bad and unloved. It had been drilled into my head through the numerous beatings and constant berating. Up to then my brother had been the only person nurturing and caring towards me, and we didn't have any issues with each other. His attitude shift also brought out a meaner side of me, a side that I've tried to contain my whole life. Anger didn't feel natural, but later on in life it became a tool that helped me to fight back and protect myself. But not then.

A single mother with a girl and two boys lived in the trailer next door to ours. They were all older than me, but that was okay. I was used to hanging out with my brother and we'd both done it all anyhow, or so I thought.

There were nights where we'd climb out of our tiny bedroom window to sneak out of the house while there were parties going on, or we'd tell our parents we were spending the night in our neighbor's camper in the back yard. One night Ryan and I went with the older boy and the girl to raid our neighbors' gardens. We had been drinking, smoking some pot, and were having some innocent fun, laughing as we ran from yard to yard scavenging for carrots or peas that we would eat right away to stave off the inevitable munchies.

We filled our pockets and jackets with the bounty of our excursion and made our way back to the camper where we would sleep that night. When we got back to the camper we hurried inside to dump our pockets of vegetables and berries into the sink. We ate our garden treasures, laughed, and smoked some more pot as the night wore on. It was late, and I was sleepy. My brother had been flirting with and making moves on the girl all night, which meant at the end of the night they bunked up together, leaving me to sleep beside the girl's sixteen-year-old brother.

I shyly lay down fully clothed and as close to the edge of the small mattress without falling off. I was uncomfortable and stiff as a board as he spooned me from behind because the last time I was this close to a male he'd hurt me. I could feel him moving around behind me before he settled in by putting his arm over me and snuggling into my backside. I heard my brother and the girl giggling as they got up and left the camper, leaving me alone with this boy. All I felt was his hot breath on the back of my neck, his body pressed too close to mine, and I didn't like it. I wrapped my arms around myself protectively and thought of bright blue skies as I pretended to sleep.

I turned over thinking it would get his breath off of my neck but it only brought us face to face and my heart skipped a beat when I realized he was naked. I sat up. He sat up too. He brushed the hair from my face and tenderly kissed my cheek as he gently held my hand to detain a getaway. I was stoned, mellow and although I was scared and confused the kissing felt nice and relaxed me. My parents looked like they enjoyed these actions happening to them so it must be what people do to show affection and I craved it.

He whispered in my ear, "You're so cute, I really like you."

I was wrapped up in a young girl's first kisses, and I knew then why the others liked it. I was floating on a cloud that was drifting through the most beautiful, blue skies I'd ever dreamed about, and I didn't want it to stop. Darkness quickly formed around the edges of that sky when he took my hands and placed them around his rigid penis and guided my hands over him. No longer mellow from the pot but wrought with fear I gasped. I did not want my hands on this boy's penis, but I couldn't pull them away from his now tighter grip as he continued to stroke himself harder. The cloud I'd been floating on disintegrated from the tears running down my face as I came crashing back to reality. He manipulated himself faster and was having trouble breathing.

I was too.

He let go of my hands and grabbed me tightly around the back of my neck. My tiny body crumpled into a heap beside him. He directed my face towards where my hands had been. He squeezed tighter on the back of my neck and growled at me to open my mouth. He held my neck with one hand and his penis with the other as he forcefully guided himself into my pursed lips. His penis exploded hot and wet liquid onto my face that dripped down onto my mouth. I quickly swiped my hand across my face. I was disgusted. I wasn't sure what'd just happened, but this definitely wasn't how I wanted to experience affection. Again though I wasn't given a choice.

He roughly pulled me down in front of him as he lay down behind me and said, "Go to sleep; it will be morning soon."

This was how I was taught about oral sex and my second sexual assault.

I was ten years old.

I never spoke about this to anyone because I was already conditioned to know that I wasn't loved, and when I got hurt it didn't matter. Who was I going to tell? Who would care or protect me?

A week later, the girl next door and I were hanging out in the shed in her back yard. It was filled with hay bales and bulky bags of seed and was where she and my brother had disappeared to the night of my assault. She and I'd never really hung out before, but I was happy to be spending some time with a girl rather than alone. She was fourteen and pretty with a smattering of freckles across her nose, crystal blue eyes, and flowing red hair. She was loud like Carrie, and I admired that about her.

We were lying beside each other on the piles of seed bags, smoking a joint when she started talking to me about Ryan and how much she liked him. We were facing each other as we smoked, and she blew it in my mouth, and as she spoke I hung on her every word. She told me in full detail the sexual things they would do to each other when they were alone. This confirmed it for me. My parents liked it, she and my brother liked it, and I was supposed to like it too. There must be something wrong with me because I didn't.

She continued to talk and mesmerize me with her soft, husky voice when I noticed her hand move. She was now cupping her own crotch in her hand and looked like she was massaging it. Just like the man at the auction had done to me. I didn't say a word to her about it. I just averted my eyes back to her face and pretended I saw nothing. She stopped and moved closer to me, her face now very close to mine. I was transfixed and intoxicated. This was nothing like the last time I was in this position.

She told me that she liked me too, not just Ryan. I wasn't used to hearing that, and I was elated knowing that someone—anyone—could like me. I was a lost little girl feeling hopeless. It'd been so long since I was shown any kind of affection from anyone that I was putty in her hands.

She gently leaned over, kissed me on the cheek, and asked, "Is it okay to kiss you?"

I didn't respond. Words had escaped me. I'd never been asked for my opinion or permission before, and I didn't know how to respond.

She lightly kissed my cheek again. Then my other cheek. Gently and slowly she slid her kiss to my neck as she caressed my arms tenderly. In those moments, I felt loved and confused. What if she hurts me like her brother? I couldn't believe I was consenting to this; although I was afraid, my feelings of being wanted and loved were stronger.

Those kisses and caresses led to intimate touching. That touching led to clothes being removed and more kissing and touching. I allowed this girl to do things to my body that I now know I shouldn't have, but she made me feel like I was special and wanted. I understood why my parents enjoyed it so much. The summer was filled with afternoons in the shed and more intimate encounters. She was my friend, she didn't hurt me, and she said she loved me. She made me laugh and feel happiness that I hadn't experienced before, and I loved her.

One afternoon she and I snuck away from everyone so that we could spend some time alone in the shed. We smoked a joint, laughed and playfully got naked as we normally did, not knowing it would be the last day we would spend in each other's company.

We were distracted by the euphoria in the energy of each other's bodies, writhing and grinding together. All of a sudden the doors to the shed flew open. My brother stood there with his mouth hinged open and his jaw almost on the ground. He looked back and forth between us. His face went red and his eyes filled with pure hatred as his brain processed what he was seeing. He barked at me to get dressed and go home then slammed the door and walked away.

I did exactly as I was told to do, as quickly as I could do it. Like the incident with her older brother, I never spoke of this to anyone

I was confused because every lesson about sexuality so far had taught me that what she and I were doing in the shed wasn't a bad thing, but Ryan didn't see it that way. He'd been pushing me aside and away for months already and finding me with the girl he'd found affection with was enough to end any kindness that remained between us. Sexuality had been shown as an open playing field, yet I felt like I'd done something wrong in finding my own healthy attention.

I was truly alone, even my body had given up on me, and soon after this I developed some bad bouts of tonsillitis. My throat and face would swell up. I couldn't swallow anything, and burned up with fever for days on end. The doctor tried different medications to control the infections, but they would repeatedly come back resulting in poor attendance at school. The good thing was that I wasn't getting hurt while I was sick; my tonsillitis kept me safe when no one else was

Pepto-Bismol Pink Walls and a White Suitcase

In 1979 I turned eleven years old. We were still living in Berwyn, Alberta, and my parents continued to live a swingers' lifestyle. They had friends in Calgary we'd go visit; my mother had been friends with the woman since her childhood. Although we were not related by blood I referred to them as my aunt and uncle. They had two: a girl and boy who were older than me which didn't matter because I wasn't a particularly social child anyhow. I'd entertain myself as the other kids would go off and do their own thing.

One night sticks out in my memory because the adults had gone out for the night and left us kids at home alone. We were all hanging out in the basement watching TV and while my brother was busy trying to make out with the girl, the older boy was trying to get touchy- feely with me. I didn't want to be around for that. I went upstairs and into the room that my parents were staying in and laid on their bed. Then being young, bored, and inquisitive, I snooped around the room. I looked in the closets and drawers and found nothing of interest. I looked under the bed and saw an old, white suitcase. I'd seen it at home in my parents' room, but had never seen what treasures hid inside.

I nervously unclipped the weathered, brass-colored latches holding it closed. I looked around to see if anyone was watching me. I was alone and lifted the lid. Inside the suitcase were several photo albums overflowing with pictures and oddly shaped toys that looked like a man's body part.

These weren't family photos I was looking at. My eyes were transfixed on hundreds of pictures of my parents engaged in sexual acts not only with each other but also in groups of three or four and more.

I recognized some of the young men. A couple of them had been to our house before but paid me no mind. They'd spend time alone laughing with my mother in her bedroom when my father wasn't home. I was told to stay in my room. My mother was so friendly and happy when they were around that I began calling them her boy toys because she seemed to like playing with them. She didn't like playing with me though; if I knocked on her door to join in the laughter, I was told to *go away.*

I wanted to laugh too, but I wasn't allowed.

In many of the photos my father was dressed up like a woman, and I was confused because he was a man, and it wasn't Halloween. The people in the pictures were mostly naked, but he was wearing different colored wigs, bras, panties, and high heels that looked silly with his beard. I was horrified and mortified, but as much as I wanted to slam down the lid and pretend it never happened, I couldn't. I was engrossed and forced myself to stare at them to prove that these were my parents, and I wasn't seeing things. I flipped through the photo albums. I was disgusted with them for engaging in such things and with myself for not closing the case sooner.

Reality check: this was what people did, and it was normal.

After I short-circuited my brain on the images, I closed it and put it back where I found it. I never spoke a word about this to anyone. Who would I have told? Finding the suitcase was more than my already overtaxed mind could handle and for years after this, I blocked it out altogether.

Around that time, I became aware that my father always had a camera in his hands taking pictures of me. I'd never noticed before and thought nothing of it as he'd ask me to smile or pose for the camera. If anything, I loved the attention.

An early bloomer, I began menstruating at eleven and my tender young breasts were budding. Those new buds got my father's attention. He would make comments disguised as jokes about the raisins, grapes, or broken fried eggs that were under my shirt, depending on my level of development. And his requests for pictures became progressively more aggressive in nature. For example, instead of saying: *Smile for daddy*, he'd say: *Lick your lips, and make them moist.*

Often he'd put down the camera, saunter up to me, and stand right in front of me. His body almost touching mine. He'd get close enough to my face that I could almost taste the beer and cigarettes on his breath. He'd look me straight in the eyes and stroke his finger along the side of my face to sweep stray hairs behind my ear. He knew that I was a quirky, awkward, introverted child, and he also knew that I loved to play dress up.

He'd ask me if I wanted to wear pretty shoes, clothes, or lipstick. Of course, being a little girl I agreed every time. I never questioned where any of the shoes or other accessories had come from. I just knew that I wanted to be pretty and feel special. They made me feel that way. He made me feel that way. I loved my daddy for that. I had no doubt in my mind back then that he loved me. As long as he showed me and told me that he did, I would do almost anything for him.

In October 1979, my dad moved our family yet again. This was the ninth move in eleven short years. This time was different from the others though because he didn't move us to some hole in the wall small town with less than 500 people in it, but to the big city of Edmonton, Alberta. And let me tell you, being in the city opened new doors for everyone in our family. Most of which should have stayed closed and some of which still remain open to this day.

Driving in our truck jammed with the few scattered contents of our lives, I read a book by Patricia Clapp titled *King of the Dollhouse* to pass the time. The story is about a little girl who felt neglected in her real life escaping into a secret world inside her dollhouse. In this imaginary world she plays with peanut butter babies and forms a relationship with the king and queen who live in her dollhouse. They establish a bond and friendship and in the end, like the story of my life, the king and queen must leave the girl. As a reminder of them, they leave her their crowns.

I connected with the little girl in the book and her need for escape because I felt neglected, lonely, and bored too. Although I didn't have a dollhouse to play with, I made do with a shoe box of fleas when I was younger, but they left me nothing; they just left.

During the drive my parents told me I would have my own room in the new house. I didn't like moving again, but the idea of having a room for me was exciting. When we first arrived in Edmonton, I was excited and apprehensive about moving to the big city because for the most part I was a farm kid.

It was a bright and sunny day when we were finally able to move into our new house. There was a small front yard with walkways leading to both the front and back doors. We had to walk up a couple of stairs to enter a small, enclosed boot room that led into the living room.

Once inside my attention was immediately drawn to the left side of the room because it looked like it was glowing. My eyes grew wide and a smile erupted across my face as I walked in and staked my claim. It was the most beautiful and girly room I'd ever seen. It had a large window where the sun could shine in and I could look out, and the walls were painted Pepto-Bismol pink.

It was perfect!

I'd never had anything pink or girly before other than Carrie's baby doll, but I hoped that this room would bring out my girly side. Besides, who else but me would want it? The color of the room may not have meant anything to a child or person who was raised in a nurturing environment, but to a broken young girl who was often picked on for looking like a boy, it symbolized the most feminine color known to female, and it was mine, all mine. I already felt like more of a girl just by standing in its florescent pink glow.

I wanted to explore and touch every nook and cranny of my new perfectly pink room. I opened the closet doors, swinging them back and forth enthusiastically. When I looked across the room, there was an old wooden grate on the floor covering the heating duct. I walked over, fascinated by the crisscross shapes, placed my hand on top, and pulled the grating out. I peered inside the dark and dusty cavity and could not believe my eyes, which must have widened to beyond saucer size. I reached my hand inside the hole and just like I was reaching into the dollhouse of my book, I grasped and pulled out two tiny, silver crowns.

My mother was standing in the doorway to my room and asked, "What'd you find?"

I sheepishly held out my hand and opened it so she could see the crowns nestled lovingly in it. In a hushed explanation I told her about the book I'd just read and about the crowns. When I was finished, we looked at each other in disbelief that I'd just found two crowns in the floor of my new perfectly pink bedroom. Finding those crowns made me feel like I wasn't alone. Someone was watching over me. Surely this was an omen from something unknown to signify there was going to be a change.

Not all of our belongings made it to our new home. We didn't own luggage so my father had us pack the things we wanted unpacked first into black garbage bags and put them in the back of the truck. Mine held most of what I possessed, which included a few toys and Baby. She was my most valuable possession; she comforted and made me feel safe every night. We didn't notice while driving but a couple of the bags must've blown off and were missing when we arrived. My bag was gone. I was saddened but carried on because the survivalist in me didn't know how else to react. I was numb.

In November I started grade six. The school was close to our house, which was good because I could walk back and forth by myself.

The school year had started a couple of months earlier, so I was yet again the new kid in my class and found it hard to make friends. The children all knew each other from previous years together and friendships were already formed that didn't allow for outsiders, especially ones like me. Since I started school late in the year, as well as my numerous absences due to tonsillitis, the teachers couldn't really grade me for that year. I passed on a hope and a prayer that I could survive grade seven.

The only thing comforting me at that time—other than my new, pink room—was that my parents were replenishing our pet population. I was accustomed to having animals around me, and it felt unnatural not to have them. They were always bringing home strays from the dump, the street, or from friends, and one day my father came home with two male Manx cats. Manx are a tailless species that originated on the Isle of Man. There was one for me with a pink bow, named Bandit, and one for my brother with a blue bow, named Digger. I was the happiest little girl in the world to have this special tabby cat with the white bib on his chest and stubby little tail.

Bandit became my new comfort and my instant best friend as he snuggled into me repeatedly and purred gently in my ears and against the hollow of my throat. He was better than a cold doll any day of the week, but I would never forget Baby.

My brother's cat however was not my best friend. A few minutes after they arrived, as I was lying on the floor reveling in cat heaven, he walked up to me, turned his back, and pissed right in my face. I let out a squeal of disgust as the hot urine splattered my no longer smiling face, forevermore harboring resentment and referring to him as *my brother's cat*.

I believe that having pets in my life eased anxieties I was experiencing and at times doubled as furry tissues collecting my tears and never minding the boogers. I didn't have anyone showing me love or affection unless it came with a hard lesson attached, but animals never asked me for anything more than a nuzzle or a scratch. Animals mattered to me, and I seemed to matter to them, which was better than nothing.

So much trauma and exposure to negative experiences left me a quiet, withdrawn, and numb little girl who you really didn't want to see pissed off. I was petite for my age, and according to the taunts that I heard on a daily basis walking to and from school, I was also poor, dirty, dressed/looked like a boy, smelled like pee, and was an ugly dog. Bandit wasn't afraid of me, so I knew that I wasn't a dog. Besides, dogs were cute.

The name-calling didn't bother me as much as when the pushing and shoving started. I had learned to stay out of the way at home, but I had to walk back and forth to school. There was no avoiding that. I was feisty but not a confrontational child and had learned to accept what was, with the hope that it would stop, if I let the bullies do what they wanted. Then it was no longer fun for them and they stopped, just like in my past. Besides, I had a brother who regularly called me *fucking dyke* under his breath. Sticks and stones were the least of my worries.

Our family dynamic changed quite a bit after this move. My father was around me much more than before, but exponentially more by the time I was mid-twelve. My mother was initially around but that became much less frequent when she discovered bingo. It was another distraction from doing what she was supposed to be doing, which was nurturing her children. Her schedule was already full with doctor appointments to get morphine shots, sexual escapades with her numerous boy toys, or stints in the psych ward. Her presence was minimal and sporadic.

Beyond these changes with my parents, within the first six months of our move to Edmonton, it was my brother's personality that had altered the most—so drastically that I barely recognized him at all. He had changed quite a bit before the move, but this was so much different. My brother hated me; he was still furious at me for what he saw with the girl from Berwyn and wanted me to pay for causing him that pain.

He was a good looking boy with dark brown hair and sparkling, baby blue eyes and was nice to everyone except me. Ryan was much more outgoing and social than I was and, people were drawn to him so he made friends easily. He was frequently out with friends; he was also drinking to excess more times than not. And although I didn't know it at the time, it was around then that he was introduced to snorting cocaine. He was fourteen.

The drugs and alcohol, fueled by his rage from the years of abuse I thought was only from our mother, was a lethal combination to say the least. When he was around, I tried to make myself scarce. I'd go into my pink room, close the door, and listen to the radio, quietly singing along. This would ease my anxiety because his previous meanness to me had escalated to cruelty and violence.

He would tell me, "You're such a stupid, waste of skin; no one wants you around, so why don't you just kill yourself?"

When words were not strong enough he would use physical violence to demonstrate how I was an aggravation, unloved, and didn't matter. The illusions of a purple sky had sealed my fate, and his beatings were validation that no blue sky was in sight. Only darkness. In that house I not only learned to avoid Ryan, but also to fear him.

I was lying in bed in my beautiful, pink bedroom trying to sleep when I heard a car pull up in the slush at the front of our house. I heard a door close and arguing. I crept over to my bedroom window, discreetly held back the corner of my curtain, and peeked to see what all the commotion was about.

It was dark and stormy outside, so I couldn't really see anything but shadows under the dim streetlight, but I could hear their angered, muffled voices through the thin glass, and one of the voices was Ryan's. They were yelling and gesturing back and forth at each other, then the driver walked to the back of his car and opened the trunk. Ryan ran towards the back of our house as the driver of the car started walking towards the house with a baseball bat in his hand.

My brother reappeared swinging a three-foot piece of chain and successfully knocked the bat out of the other boy's grasp. I watched as he beat the boy within an inch of his life, blood spattering on the snow. It was clear to me that the boy who had once protected me was gone. He didn't care anymore; no one cared. The thing I didn't know was that this was just the beginning and that his anger was not selective.

In December 1979 through some stroke of genius, someone who worked for the Provincial Government of Alberta decided that my parents were fit and mentally capable enough to allow handicapped infants and children enter our home as foster children.

Now keep in mind that this had been at least the ninth time we'd moved in eleven years. My mother had spent the better part of my childhood viciously beating and berating my brother and me when she was around. When she wasn't, she was in and out of psychiatric wards or lying in bed in a prescription drug induced state—pretty much the same thing. The only difference is that facilities offered her three square meals a day and a sponge bath, and I didn't.

My father was in and out of jail or outrunning the law, keeping us on the move, and had two neglected and abused children of his own who'd been in government care. Yes, these people were *perfect* candidates! Please, bring on the paycheck...ahem, I mean the children.

For a woman who told me numerous times that she should've aborted me, my mother seemed happy to receive the paycheck more than the children into our family of horrors. This new development signified once again some very big changes.

A total of five children came and stayed with us in the first six months after our home passed approval. They ranged in age from a couple of days old to three years old and all were special needs children. It was a chaotic environment of babies crying, feedings, diaper changes, and baby giggles. Each child was unique, demanding, and touched my life in their own ways. I learned and became attached to all of them quickly through playing with and helping to care for them. I loved the distraction that music allowed and would quietly sing for the children along with the radio.

When they cried I'd snuggle them softly like Baby and sing "You Are My Sunshine." I would smile at good memories of my first friend, Carrie, as I soothed their baby tears with my own. Tears of joy because having the innocence of children in my life showed me that I could love and be loved back. It gave me hope for a day when I would have my own children that I could love unconditionally.

The Whip of a Tongue and How to Lash It

The first child who entered my life in that house changed me forever. His name was Paul, and on that day when I looked into those monstrous blue eyes of his it was instant love for me. He was a chubby, eighteen-month-old who couldn't walk or talk yet, but he was close. I listened to the social worker tell my parents that he had cerebral palsy and epilepsy and that his biological parents were brother and sister, so there were other possible genetic complications as well. They were told to give him quality of life because quantity probably wasn't an option. We certainly didn't have quality of life and the measure of care, whether emotional or physical, was inadequate at best.

Despite my own lack of parental guidance, I naturally stepped into a maternal role with him and the other children. I didn't know any different; I'd been taking care of myself and the motherly duties of the house my whole life. When Paul cried or wanted attention, I was the one who gave it to him. When he had dirty diapers, I changed them. I may have worn rubber gloves and a mask and snorkel set to get through it, but he got changed no worse for wear. My funny look kept him entertained during these frequent diaper changings, making my job easier. I learned quickly that babies poop a lot, something even more apparent with more than one baby in the house.

Paul and I were spending all of our time together and being under my wing he soon learned how to walk, talk, and was potty-trained. He loved all the music I played for him and loved singing even more than listening. We spent hours listening to records or the radio and singing along. If we didn't know the words, we'd hum because there's a lot to be said for some killer humming.

My mother did try to step up to the plate and act like a normal human being when the children first arrived. She stayed present long enough to teach me the essentials of childcare and to coo at innocence. I didn't need her help though. I already knew how to care for a child, because I essentially raised myself. The love, affection, and protection that I never received from her, I selflessly gave to those smaller than me. I was tough on the outside, but through my caretaking, on the inside I was a little girl who finally felt joy instead of pain.

Although caretaking energized me, it didn't very take long for the neediness of sick babies to wear on my mother, and her addictions took precedence once again. She became mentally unavailable, detached, and departed back to la-la-land in her bedroom. This left me the sole maternal figure in my parents' absence, mental or otherwise.

My father did most of the cooking and I watched him closely so I could copy the things he made. I taught myself how to cook so that everyone could eat when he wasn't around. It was during my mother's brief lapses of sanity that my relationship with my father launched into uncharted territory. I called him Dad or Daddy then. As I celebrated my twelfth birthday, I was content not only playing mother and house with the children to nurture, but also with my daddy's attention.

With the new school year came a new torment of insults by some of the neighborhood kids; however, I wasn't alone anymore. I'd emerged from my solitude because of the children in my care. This new role allowed me to make a couple of friends in the neighborhood. We would take the little ones outside to play at the park where we would sing and be children. In those moments, I was happy because I felt loved.

I started grade seven and my teacher's name was Mr. Engels. One day after school I stayed late because some kids were picking on me before last bell. I didn't want to face the torment, so I stayed behind. I hid in the girl's bathroom until I heard enchanting music reverberating off the inside walls of the cubicle and was compelled to discover what it was. The captivating music was coming from my classroom; my teacher Mr. Engels was playing the piano. A couple of other children stood beside the piano listening.

I walked over to them and stood there silently until he finished. I said, "That was beautiful. What's the name of it?"

He said, *"Music Box Dancer."*

I loved the title and the music. I'd emotionally connected with music and the lyrics of songs since Carrie's influence and loved listening to it almost as much as reading. I found escape in the words and the feelings behind them, especially in the case of uplifting songs, and how they allowed me to feel positive emotions. Carrie had been my spot of sunshine when skies were not blue and had given me a glimpse of joy. To make up for stealing her baby doll and the childhood she'd lost, I had decided to share music with the children in my care.

That day in Mr. Engels' classroom, I felt so drawn to *Music Box Dancer*. I'd never heard anything as happy and light before. With a large smile on my face, I asked, "Can you please play it again?"

He said yes and when he finished playing it for the second time, he looked at us. "You should all head on home because I don't want your parents to worry."

Under my breath, I whispered, "Mine won't."

Before I walked out the door, he stopped me and asked if I wanted to clap out the blackboard erasers because he didn't have time. I jumped at the chance to stay in the sanctity of the classroom for just a little bit longer. When I was done I looked at him, thanked him, and walked home hoping that my journey would be a safer one because the other kids who bullied me would be home already. The music and kindness of Mr. Engels had offered me joy and protection. Music remains a source of peace in my life.

School however, remained a place of fear due to the bullies, and I avoided attending. Because of the help I provided caring for the foster children, my parents didn't object to me staying away from school.

We needed more space for cribs and bunk beds upstairs to accommodate the flow of children so I was ousted from my beautiful, pink room to the dark, dank basement. I didn't welcome the move, but I didn't have a choice. Downstairs had two adjoined rooms with no physical doors, only threadbare sheets held up with thumb-tacks to protect me from an angry and violent brother in the next room.

My room was at the front of the space so my brother would literally walk through my space to get to his. I had a small, single cot bed that was positioned against the wall right underneath a small storm drain window. I liked this because I could see what time of day it was or if someone was walking by. Unfortunately, blue skies didn't last for long periods in my life, and shortly after my move to the basement my brother sexually assaulted me for the first time.

That night I was lying in bed with my body pressed close enough to the side of the wall that I felt invisible under a rumple of blanket, but not close enough that spiders could crawl on me. My eyes were closed when I felt a movement on the bed behind me. In my heart I hoped it was my cat coming to snuggle with me, but experience and prevailing purple skies knew it wasn't. The weight was too much for it to be Bandit and there was only one other option; my brother had left his room.

I pretended to be asleep, praying that he would just go back to his room and leave me alone, when I felt his hand snake around and quickly cover my mouth.

He hissed at me to be quiet and told me he had a lesson for me that I needed to learn. He nastily brought up the position he'd caught me in the shed with the girl from Berwyn and roughly demonstrated how oral sex was supposed to be done, on me.

Before leaving my bed that night he placed his hands around my throat and issued a hushed warning about the consequences of talking, and I was quite secure in the fact that he wouldn't have a problem carrying those warnings out. Lesson learned.

I shoved down my feelings and went on about life as if nothing had happened, which was what I'd been taught since birth. Although others mattered to me and I craved attention, it was clear that I still didn't matter or deserve protecting. It was oddly familiar and comforting to feel pain—and foreign to feel joy—but it was the only way I knew.

To escape the confines of my new hell, I tried going back to school on a more regular basis. It was even more of a challenge for me faced with this new "lesson" that I'd been taught. Going to school meant I was leaving the children with my mother unprotected, but I needed an escape.

I shared the classroom with the same kids as the year before. They had learned I didn't fight back, so they stopped picking on me for the most part—until I started taking the foster children outside. This gave them new ammunition to hurl in my direction, and I became *the girl who lives with retards*. The kids in the city were meaner, and more aggressive with their meanness, than farm kids ever were. I was tough though. I could handle them.

The only problem with the new taunt was that they weren't attacking me anymore but little children who didn't ask to come into this world the way they had. I wasn't about to stand around and let it happen. I discovered something bigger than myself, a feeling I'd only felt towards animals before: compassion for those who couldn't defend themselves. I wasn't as big as the nurturing mother bear protecting her cubs from lurking danger, but I was much more ferocious because I was taught the whip of a tongue and how to lash it.

Heaven knows I had enough adult on my plate already as I struggled and juggled taking care of everyone but myself, but now I was forced to add a new element to my repertoire: fighting.

One evening after school I talked with my father about the bullying that was going on at school, and what he taught me that day became valuable words of wisdom.

He said, "If you don't want the other kids to fuck with you, you need to walk up to the biggest bitch in the school and knock her the fuck out. Problem solved."

This was my first and only lesson on how to get the other kids to stop bullying me, taught to me by a man who intimidated everyone. If I bullied first, I wouldn't be bullied. This didn't sound like the best plan to solve my problem, but he was my father, and he knew best. I didn't want to hit like I had been, but I knew violence was something that kept people away, and so I learned how to fight.

I was already unpopular and this new technique, when put to use, made me even less popular. It also torpedoed my plan to attend school regularly.

One of my first uses of this violence was to settle a score with a couple of girls I had thought were my friends. A cruel incident later proved those friendships to be a façade and damned them to a beating. It wouldn't be the last thumping I handed out.

One of the girls was named Dorothy. She lived in a tall, blue house, and I'd climb the long front stairs in the mornings to pick her up for school. I loved entering her home, which smelled of fresh oranges and warm oatmeal with cinnamon. I'd walk into her front hallway, inhale deeply, and hold in the delicious aromas. My house never smelled like hers. It was heavenly. It didn't even bother me if she was late or if I found out she'd already left with other friends—some of whom didn't have much need for me to even be in their basic vicinity—because at least I got to start the day with that nurturing fragrance.

One sunny, winter day I called Dorothy and invited her over to my house so I could show her a new outfit I'd gotten. It was stretchy, purple and white checkered, polyester, bell-bottomed overalls jumpsuit. I'd found it in a bag of clothing one of our neighbors donated to help our family out.

I couldn't wait to show it off to the girl I believed was my friend. It made no difference to me that it wasn't actually new. It was new to me, and that was all that mattered. Coming from a neighbor was always better than treasure diving at the dump. I adored my jumper. It was pretty and girly and oh so purple. Not to mention, I thought looked really cool wearing it. It was a huge step up from wearing my brother's hand-me-downs and being mistaken for an ill-dressed boy.

She agreed to come over, and I excitedly put on my new jumper. I wanted to parade around my front entrance in the pink sunshine glow that my old room provided. I desired validation from my friend that I was a pretty little girl just like her and the others. When the bell rang I ran to the door as quickly as my little feet could carry me. Paul was right on my tail. He wanted to see what all the excitement was about. I flung the door open with such grandeur that I almost fell over from the swift motion.

To my surprise, there were three girls standing there, not one. She'd brought two friends along. She explained that they'd met on the way to my house, she told them about my new jumper, and they wanted to see too. I was ecstatic. I invited them into the enclosed porch of the house to get them out of the cold.

I wanted to make sure that the girls got an eyeful of my pretty jumper so I asked them if they wanted some water to drink.

One of the girls said yes, so I sauntered away from them into the kitchen. It wasn't even thirty seconds after I turned my back that I heard Paul scream out in pain and begin to cry. I ran back to the door to find the girls laughing with each other.

I asked, "What happened to him?"

They all feigned ignorance and shrugged as they continued to giggle under their breath. I was irritated by this but told them to leave so that I could console Paul. He was a smart cookie and although he couldn't talk yet, he understood what was being said to him.

I asked him, "Did you get a boo-boo? Point to where you're hurt, buddy."

I expected him to point to his tummy or bottom indicating an ache or cramp. Instead he looked at me with tears brimming out of his big blue eyes and reached around and touched the back of his pudgy little arm. I took off his shirt and discovered a large, angry, red welt where he pointed. It looked like someone had pinched him. Hard. I was sad, stunned, and appalled. I couldn't wrap my head around someone being so cruel to a child simply because he was different from them. I rationalized that it was okay for bad things to happen to me, but it wasn't okay for it to happen to him.

And that's when I got angry.

This was a new feeling. This particular kind of anger. Protective anger. How dare these girls hurt someone I loved. It was fine if they called *me* names or tried to hurt *me* because I could defend myself but not Paul. He was an innocent child I loved and who loved me back. Hurting him was a big mistake on their part. They had stupidly put themselves in the crosshairs of my built up vengeance.

I'd never been in an actual fistfight before but this was enough to throw me into the ring. This was the motivational catalyst that allowed me to hurl myself headlong into doling out justice. Finally, I had had enough. I was too angry to deal with it immediately and didn't want Paul to see that anger so I temporarily pushed it down.

The next morning, I marched to school with a new feistiness. I wasn't the timid girl I was the day before. Today I was angry as a wet hornet. I steeled myself and approached the three girls who stood in a group.

I matched their gaze and warned them, "Watch out for me after school."

And then I walked away trying to look as tough as I could. Though I was vigilant and determined, I was also scared and hesitant. It wasn't in my nature to want to hit people. It was usually me getting hit. And though no one had ever defended me, I was compelled to do what I had to do to defend Paul.

I didn't know whose ass I was going to kick first. Only one of these girls had hurt Paul, but they were all going to pay. One girl did the deed and the other two were defending it. In my opinion they were all guilty and punishable.

I eventually decided that it would be Dorothy who'd go down first. The word had gotten around about my warning and all of our classmates and her friends were anticipating the fistfight between her and me. To prepare for the fight, the kids used their lunch hour to take snow and ice balls to construct a boxing circle for us to tussle in after school.

The last bell rang, and we all met at the circumference of the ring. I took my mittens off and removed a splint off one of my fingers—it had been broken two days earlier trying to protect my head from my brother's roundhouse kick. I didn't want to be accused of chickening out or scratching her when all I wanted to do was punch this girl's face off.

We glared at each other and I said, "I'm going to kick your ass for hurting Paul"

I wanted my intent clear. Someone from behind shoved me into her, and I punched uncontrollably, swinging blindly, and wrestled her to the ground. This displeased the gallery of onlookers who promptly picked up the ice balls and pelted them at my head and body. That ended the fight and I ran home in complete and utter hysterics.

It may not have looked like it to any of them, but in my eyes that was a victory. I had defended Paul and felt less angry.

I stayed home from school the next day to plan my next attack, and I wasn't ready to face the angry mob yet. I waited until the end of the school day then walked to the second girl's house. I knew she had to pass by the back alley to get to her house and that's where I waited. I saw her approach. I jumped out from my hiding spot and tossed her to the ground. I punched her repeatedly not making a sound until I felt better inside and then left like I wasn't even there.

That same night I received a phone call from the third girl. Before I could even say hello she blurted out "It wasn't me! It was Dorothy, she pinched Paul. Please don't beat me up. We can be friends instead."

I was happy to hear the truth, and fighting wasn't how I wanted to live my life, so I decided to grant her request. She could keep her friendship though. I didn't want or need it. Anyone who would stand by and watch that happen had no place in my life. I still had a couple of other friends in the neighborhood, the love of a special little boy and my cat.

Another lesson was learned and set firmly in place showing me that I was doing it all wrong before. I'd been nice to people because I wanted them to like me. That was how it was supposed to work. But my father and past life experiences taught me that violence and aggression were more effective ways to get attention.

I failed grade seven that year with forty-six absences in one term alone. My teacher and parents didn't feel like I'd do well in grade eight so they all made the choice to hold me back a year. Another confirmation that I was stupid and my opinion didn't count. No matter though; I preferred to stay home with Paul anyhow. He didn't hit me or make me feel like I was less than nothing.

I quickly grew to love Paul deeply, which healed my heart enough to want to survive. He helped me feel something other than pain and neglect, something I hadn't experienced in a long time. It's hard for me to realize that at twelve I had so much darkness in my heart and head. Some days it was as though I simply existed on a cellular level, drifting in and out of my days alone in the world, masking my pain with cigarettes, marijuana, and alcohol.

I wish I could say that I quit all of my vices when Paul came into my life, but I'd be lying. However, the fact that I was now needed and my affection reciprocated did decrease my intake to a bare minimum. I found a new drug that felt better than all of the others combined: love. I was hooked. Finally, my loving nature that I'd pushed down for so long was beginning to bubble to the surface and touch others.

Showing and sharing that love with Paul became a ritual on a daily basis. Every night when I'd put him to bed I'd say, "Good night. Sweet dreams. I love you. See you in the morning."

It was not only validation for him that he wasn't alone, but that I wasn't alone anymore either. This simple phrase gave us something to look forward to.

Photographs

10 months old before my smile was suppressed.

12 months old and my affection for animals is already evident.

18 months old and I was already familiar and comfortable with
motorcycles.

My brother Ryan and I at ages 8 & 5 before our relationship was tarnished by abuse and addiction.

Survivalist 101

Still, I was starving for affection, so when my father would ask me to spend time with him, I'd jump at the chance. My mother was also more aware of her surroundings than usual and she'd stay with the children while I'd go off with my father.

He took me to a gun range where I practiced target shooting with my pellet gun that progressed to a .22 rifle. Since Onoway, I'd been familiar with guns and was always a pretty good shot. I was proud of this because I'd felt inadequate so much of the time. Being good at something was a relief.

One day while we were at the gun club my father told me that he had a surprise for me, and it was one that I'd waited a long time for. He'd brought his most prized possession to the shooting range that day and was going to let me fire off a round. I was overjoyed. He brandished his weapon in the air and then gently placed it in my delicate hands. As the extended barreled, stainless steel .44 magnum handgun touched my trembling hands the cold was electric. I felt so powerful standing there with this beautiful monster in my grasp. I'd seen the gun around the house and was beside myself with excitement knowing that I was finally going to shoot it. I felt special because he didn't let anyone touch his gun, and here it was in my hands.

I stood there, a waif of a girl, holding a pistol that was almost as big as I was. Exhilaration and strength surge through my body as I pulled that trigger but nothing happened. I braced my tiny legs and arms again and focused every ounce of willpower and determination into the trigger and *kaboom*...I flew backwards through the air. During my excitement, I failed to pull the hammer back and fired the gun dry. It was a rookie mistake that resulted in me getting knocked onto my skinny little ass and my earphones flying off of my head.

I'm not sure how far backwards I flew, but I knew I was not standing in the same spot anymore. Although I didn't hit the target that day, it didn't matter because I was so hyped up on adrenaline from the kick of the gun that I think I laughed nervously for the next three days.

On that day, as he helped me up off the ground and dusted me off, my father kissed me on the lips for the first time. His tongue brushed my lower lip. I was surprised at first but then rationalized that it was just to show me how proud of me he was. I thought nothing more of it after that. He was my dad and he was nice to me. It was normal to kiss your twelve-year old daughter with tongue on the mouth, right?

In July and August of 1980, my father and I were pretty much inseparable, and I reveled in the attention that he was giving me. I thought that if I was spending time with him, I'd be safe from the grasp of my brother.

My dad introduced me to an event called a *black powder rendezvous*, which opened up a whole new world to me. People dressed up like cowboys and Indians and slept in teepees. There were competitions with cannons, bows and arrows, black powder guns, and hatchets to win prizes. I advanced from firing rifles and handguns to throwing hatchets and knives, and my accuracy continued to excel. I loved dressing up, being outdoors with Mother Nature, and the attention and love I was getting from my father.

We spent hours together at a work station he built in the basement where he educated me on skills that I couldn't learn in school. I'd help him melt down lead and pour it into molds to make ammunition for the black powder guns we would shoot. I learned how to intricately loom beads together, cut bone, and create beautiful jewelry that I would wear.

He and I went for drives out to the country, often making stops to scrape up road kill. I learned that finding death on the road provided some supplies we needed that we couldn't buy at the store. We gathered porcupine quills, bird bones, eagle feathers, deer antlers, and bear claws, but sometimes if the kill was fresh he'd bring it home and cook it for dinner.

Road kill venison roast, anyone?

It didn't matter to me, food was food, and it was more meat than a squirrel.

My costume was as a First Nations princess. It was a floor length, creamy white, doeskin dress with a luxuriously silky lining. It was adorned with elaborate beading and fringes on the bottom that tickled my toes. My dad would style my hair into two frizzy, blonde, wispy braids, each fashioned with a bald eagle feather. Around my head I proudly wore bands and rows of colorful beads in zigzag designs that I'd spent hours meticulously hand-beading on a loom. My neck was caressed by a choker I'd made with hollowed out and polished bird bones, layered with porcupine quills, separated by cross sections of deer antler.

To complete my outfit on my feet were mukluks of the softest doeskin with complicated beading and fringes. While creating I was able to put love and attention to detail into the jewelry and the praise from my dad reinforced my feeling of being capable. While I was dressed up I felt pretty and my father made me feel that way, so I adored him for that. He continued to document my prettiness, and the pictures he took of me documented the changing nature of our relationship.

His pictures also showed my transition from a little girl to a young woman. I grew small breasts and started to develop hips. As I matured the style of his pictures became more adult in nature. The changes in me were natural; his chronicle of them, I'd come to understand, was inappropriate.

The more my father showered me with adoration and affection, the more my mother's hatred for me was received with every glare in my direction. So even though I seemed to be gaining something, I was also losing something—the hope of having my mother's affection.

My parents continued with their open relationship, so a flow of people came and went through the house and their bedroom. For my mother, men of all ages, shapes, and sizes appeared when my father wasn't around. My father was no better as I watched, unseen, as his own string of lovers came and went. Paul was now in the pink room that used to be mine, and because it was right beside theirs, I did my best to distract him from the activities. We would go in and close the door to play and listen to loud music.

It was normal to us. Life as usual.

Wheat Fields Taken Away

I'd been taking care of Paul full-time for almost a year and a half, and our bond was undeniable and unbreakable as we spent every waking moment together. I was protecting him from the harsh realities of life but wasn't able to protect myself from the physical, emotional, and psychological torments that Ryan continued to batter me with.

Life became less hectic for me once Paul was the only child who remained in our care, the other children moving on to permanent homes. I didn't realize it at the time, but he and I essentially had a mother-child relationship, one that I craved from my own mother but never received. I was the only responsible person in the house, and I was raising him like he was my own child.

A few times he mistakenly called me Mom, but I always corrected him. "I'm your sister."

The parade of derelicts traipsing through my parents' bedroom had tapered off for the most part. My relationship with my mother remained strained, her glares at me radiating irritation. Her animosity was almost palpable when she saw me laughing or having fun with her husband. She was using bingo as a full-time vice instead of men, because what better way to spend the government's money than in a bingo hall, right? Out gambling while her abused and neglected teen daughter cared for the child that she was being paid to raise?

Life was livable because of Paul and my father. My mother became present and coherent and we functioned as a family—a dysfunctional one, but still the only family I knew.

One evening after a night of partying, I could smell my brother as he walked through my room to his. He was sobbing, and my heart physically ached when I heard anyone crying. I naively entered his space, drawn by the vulnerability in his sobs and knowing how it felt to be alone during those times. My head told me not to go, but my heart was good and hoped that somewhere inside Ryan there was goodness too.

There was not. The light inside of me was shining and my brother quickly snuffed it out. Just like the neighbor boy in the camper when I was ten years old, my brother violently forced me to have oral sex with him.

When he was finished he seethed, "You're pathetic and disgusting, and I want you to think about what a whore you are. Now go to bed."

After that, Ryan's presence in the house became less frequent and life inside got easier. It was life outside of the house that had to watch out for me because I was pissed off.

I was sporadically attending a different school, which was much further to get to and harder to get away from. I failed grade seven and was trying to avoid the taunts and humiliation of that; I already knew I was a failure, and I didn't need anyone else pointing that fact out to me. I decided to follow my dad's advice once again on how to deal with bullies and entered swinging.

The first day at my new school, I walked up to the biggest girl I could find and punched her square in the face. What father hadn't told me was that the biggest girl doesn't necessarily mean the toughest girl. In this case, they were best friends, and I'd pissed them both off. I stayed away from school for a few days after this, hoping when I returned no one would notice or recognize me.

They did and I faced the consequences of listening to my father's sage advice.

The girls' best friend and I met that day in a back alley by the school at lunch break. It was a cool day outside, and I was wearing a bright yellow coat. There was a semi-circle of people waiting to see us kick the snot out of each other and I was troubled. There had been enough hitting and fighting in my life. I just wanted it to stop, but I couldn't back down now. I'd made my bed, now I would lie in it.

I started to take my coat off so I wouldn't be restrained. Someone from behind grabbed my arms and held them tightly as the girl I was going to fight lunged at me. She grabbed me by the hair and twisted it into her fist. Filled with rage, I wrenched my body around and was able to shrug off the person holding my arms. Then I wrestled my attacker to the ground and punched her in the face to release my pent up storm clouds.

It wasn't her I was angry at or even her face that I was smashing. As I hit her I pictured every person in my life who'd hurt or belittled me, proving that I was stronger than them. I could protect myself now and didn't need anyone else to do it.

The outlet of fury that I experienced in that moment quenched a thirst that I didn't know I possessed and scared me to death. It was all over before it began because someone grabbed me from behind and pulled me off the girl. I kicked and punched at the air that now separated us until I realized where I was.

A man set me down on my feet and yelled at me "Go home!" as he walked away. Everyone else had scrambled already as I stood there alone and sobbed uncontrollably at my frustration.

School wasn't a priority for me, and my parents were getting calls about me fighting and not attending classes, so they sat me down to have a parent-child talk.

They berated me for the way I was living my life—the life I was taught to live—and I got mad. I knew why I was lashing out. As my parents, shouldn't they? I wasn't fighting and skipping school to drink and smoke pot because I lived a happy existence. I thought it was time for some truth, as scared as I was to tell it. The repercussions couldn't be any worse than the lessons taught during my assaults.

The conversation wasn't what they expected. I divulged what had happened with my brother. I was on an emotional downward spiral and could see no light. There was no one else in life I could talk to, and I hoped they would do something to help the desperate situation I was in. I was vulnerable and alone, and I needed a mother bear's protection provided by someone other than myself. I didn't realize they were incapable of that protection, so I might as well have kept it to myself.

Their solution was saying it would be dealt with and that was the end of that. Ryan never sexually assaulted me again, but it was only because I didn't put myself in a situation where he could. I knew that my parent hadn't done anything because Ryan didn't follow through with his threats. He was always quick to remind me that if I did or said anything about what had happened it would be my demise. Although my sky was dark I wasn't ready to leave this world yet. I deeply harbored hopes and dreams of a life with my own children one day, and Paul still needed me. Ryan's blatant threats throughout my life meant I was constantly looking over my shoulder, waiting for his revenge.

I continued to grow closer to my father even though he was busy with a friend at the time preparing to open up a motorcycle repair-chop shop in Leduc, Alberta. This is the first and only time in my life where we actually acted as a cohesive family outside of the house. Our entire family was doing things together like taking road trips to British Columbia and riding dune buggies out in the country with my father's new friends. We were laughing and having fun together which was quite the switch from hiding in our bedrooms.

I thought to myself that maybe telling them was the best decision I'd made. I felt lighter not carrying the full weight of my assaults, but the threat of my brother was still real and inevitable. We spent time at the shop together even if sometimes it was quite boring for a thirteen-year-old girl and her four-year-old counterpart.

In the summer of 1981, I somehow managed to successfully pass grade seven despite my continued absences due to caring for Paul and my bouts with tonsillitis. My father's shop was open full-time now, and business was booming. He decided that he needed to be closer to the business and moved us again for the tenth time in thirteen years. Thankfully we moved back to the country, a little farm in Calmar, Alberta. Ryan decided to stay in the city, which was a bonus for my sanity.

It didn't take long for my dad to provide us with animals and pets that I desired, which kept Paul and I busy. Our mornings were filled with collecting eggs while feeding and running with the chickens, ducks, and goats. In the afternoons he and I would spend hours hanging out in and around the barn where we could pet and feed my horse Shannon, Wilbur the pig, Daisy the calf, and whatever other creatures may be lurking in there. My father had a knack for bringing home the coolest and most extraordinary animals that I could've only dreamed about seeing at a zoo, let alone in my own barn.

For a time, we had a de-scented skunk named Lil' Stinker and a fluffy and inquisitive snowy owl with the most intriguing yellow eyes that we named, quite fittingly, Useless. He was an abandoned, young owl with zero hunting skills and a broken wing. We even had to smack his live mouse dinner on the head to kill it before he would eat it. He was injured and needed a place to rehabilitate, and I was happy that my dad had picked our house for that to happen. It was ironic that our house was a refuse for Useless to heal, while it was the place that often brought me torment.

Being back on the farm with space to run and connect with nature, bugs, and animals was good for my heart and offered smatterings of healing blue sky. I was drawn to the unwavering and rejuvenating spirit that animals possessed and I taught Paul to appreciate them too.

Life became fairly simple and much easier for me considering my experiences thus far. I was a nice girl who loved to laugh, but I also had a hair trigger to my anger when it came to protecting Paul. Any reference to him being different in a bad way sent me off the deep end. Yes, he was different. He loved me and never raised a hand or said a belittling word to me. He was like my own child that needed protecting, which I did voraciously.

I have to admit the move to Calmar and the success of the shop did wonders for our family that summer. I was convinced that life was finally going to change with my brother gone and my mother and father both present and accounted for. There was no bingo out there and my mother actually took a working role as we functioned together to raise Paul. Her dislike for me was still apparent, but she seemed to tolerate my presence more during this family time.

My father worked as a mechanic and was constantly building or tinkering with some type of vehicle or another, and sometimes I'd help him. He'd ask me to hand him a wrench or other tool, and over time I learned the right ones for the job. It was summer so I didn't have school and was hanging around with my father and his biker friends more often than not. Paul and I would play together or sing upstairs in the office, or I would be by my father's side smoking a joint and twisting wrenches. During this time, we all assisted in building a badass V8 trike from the ground up.

She was a one of a kind, sleek machine. He'd give us rides, driving around aimlessly for hours on end. I was free, comfortable, and felt safe riding on the back of a motorcycle behind him because I grew up there. One weekend we shined up the beautiful beast of twisted metal and entered it into a car show and competition at Northlands Agricom to see if we could win anything.

He and I both scored prize's that day. He won a huge first place trophy that was almost as tall as me. I went home with an autographed picture of Lou Ferrigno, who was the original *Incredible Hulk.* He was at the car show making an appearance and invited me to sit and talk with him during lunch. He was super friendly and made me laugh during our short time together. He seemed to think I mattered. My prize was much more valuable and made for a pretty cool day and bragging rights. I had the picture to prove it!

My father frequently asked if I wanted to go for rides on the trike, and I always did. That led to many road trips back and forth to Edmonton and surrounding areas, just for the sake of driving. I'd sit on the back, get high, and lose myself in the wind as it whipped across my smiling face. She was a head-turner with her fat back tires and her extended, forked frame, and I felt special riding on her. I was important and people were noticing me.

I was getting attention too because I was wearing Daisy Duke short-shorts and teeny, tiny bikini tops as my father instructed. I wanted people to know I was a girl and they did. More like a scantily clad, fully developed, grown woman, although in reality I was a fourteen-year-old child growing up a victim of illusions.

My mother retreated back to depression, prescription abuse, and hospital visits that left Paul back in my care and me in my father's. Before I started referring to him as *my father*, I used *dad* and our relationship had grown into something I could then only describe as the perfect daddy-daughter relationship. I knew without a doubt that he had affection for me, and I doted on his every word because I loved my daddy. I trusted him with every fiber of my being and believed his words of praise to be true. He gave me the attention that I'd been craving my whole life, and all I was required to do was wear small clothes in order to get it.

He would regularly tell me how fucking hot I looked or that my tits and ass were filling in nicely, and I thought nothing of it. People as a rule didn't say nice things to me, and I thought he was complimenting me. Attention is attention whether it is positive or negative, and I was eating up the lines of shit he was feeding me.

His camera appeared more regularly as he took this new country backdrop as an opportunity to take more photos. One afternoon he told me that he wanted to take some pictures of me and styled my hair into to high pigtails on the sides of my head that bounced playfully when I walked, He then applied a coat of mascara and a smudge Vaseline for my lips. He drove the trike out into the wheat field behind the barn where I would occasionally play hide-and-seek with Paul or escape to for solitude. We went as far as he could go without getting stuck and then handed me the smallest red and white bikini that I'd ever seen. He told me he would turn around while I changed and as cold and uncomfortable as I was, I did it. What other choice did I have?

Besides, we were out in the middle of a wheat field where no one could see me. What could be seen however, were my breasts and everything else in between and below. The bottom of the cup width adjusted on the string, and after he was finished "adjusting" my top, my nipples were barely covered by a scant slip of material and the bottoms weren't much bigger.

He encouraged me to straddle and sprawl myself against the wheat stalks, ground, and trike in various seductive positions like the women on the front of his *Easy Rider* magazines. I did this without question because I had no reason to doubt that everything was the way it was supposed to be. By that time, my sense of what should be was so convoluted that I accepted and acquiesced despite the knot in my stomach telling me otherwise. Although someone else would have clearly seen the blue sky above me, it was completely blocked from my view, and I saw darkness.

When he finished taking pictures out there, he drove the trike into the barn because what fourteen-year-old farm girl didn't straddle a hunk of metal in a nonexistent bikini inside a barn too?

As I look back at that period of my life now, it disgusts me. At the time I didn't think anything of it because in my world this was considered normal. Where I once thought of the wheat field as a carefree and special hiding place where I could lay unnoticed and listen to nature move around me; after that day, I never returned.

I wasn't the only youthful victim of my father's photo compulsion. Over the years he took thousands of pictures of me as well as any female that had the misfortune of becoming my friend and following me into his lair. I never thought anything of it because having pictures taken had always been a prevalent part of my life. It was how he demonstrated and voiced his affection towards me. Although I didn't understand what his fascination was with me, I allowed the photos to happen because it made him happy. I wasn't a particularly pretty or skinny girl. I thought I was barely noticeable compared to other girls, but he told me I was pretty.

Even though I was objectified, I had body issues. I thought my thighs and butt were too dimpled and jiggly and my belly wasn't flat enough. I mentioned my concerns to my father, and he suggested a new form of sit-ups he'd said he'd learned from a friend. He told me that I would have rock hard abs and legs in no time if I was diligent with these sit-ups. I followed his instruction because I believe he wanted to help me and thought nothing of it.

When intoxicated, my mother would remind me that I was ugly and good for nothing, so it was a nice change to hear about my good qualities like my full lips, tits, and ass.

Like a Chicken with Its Head Cut Off

The summer of 1982 inevitably turned to fall, and I began attending grade eight in Calmar. I was once again the new kid who was socially dysfunctional and had a huge chip on her shoulder. I co-existed with Paul and my father at that point because they were the only two I thought hadn't wronged me, and I didn't know anyone else. I could immediately feel that this place was different and a whole other experience compared to what I was used to. It was a small school where in the hallways the children and teachers would say hello as they passed each other, not walk by blindly.

I was anxious and defensive when I first walked into the classroom but was greeted by a group of smiling, friendly, and non-judgmental girls my age. They didn't want to fight me. They were friendly and welcomed me into their group. This was a new concept for me, one I hadn't experienced before as a new kid but enjoyed very much. I found a peaceful place with these girls and decided there was no need to knock anyone the fuck out. They saw me for whom I was inside and not for what I'd been through on the outside. I had an iron clad outer coating but was still a vulnerable little girl underneath that required acceptance.

I was a good girl at school for the most part because while away from the house, I didn't feel the need to escape into a world of intoxication. None of the innocent country girls smoked, drank, or smoked pot. I tried a couple of times to sway a few to my less-than-innocent ways but they weren't having it and kindly refused. In an effort to fit in, I cut down to only smoking cigarettes, which strikes me as an odd thing to write considering my age at the time.

I felt like the teachers cared about me learning, and I tried to focus and pay attention in class but found it difficult. It didn't take me long to discover the school's library, where I would spend my free time. I was an enthusiastic reader. Sometimes the words looked mixed-up but I loved the smell and heft of books and the sanctuary they provided. I'd get lost in adventures or learn something new; it was my choice. It was the one thing in life that I had control over. Everything else was decided for me. If I didn't like a story, I could close the cover. I couldn't close the cover of my life.

Stories with heroines were a particular favorite but I'd devour any book that I could get my hands on including encyclopedias. I invented a word game that I'd play when I couldn't find anything else to read other than my dictionary. I'd randomly flip through the pages, letting my finger stop where it may, and blindly point to a word on the page. The challenge of the game was to use it in proper context twice in a day, whether that was in my head or out loud. One of my favorite words to find was *filipendulous*, which meant being suspended or strung up by a single thread, and I related to how that felt.

Books were a way for me to escape my reality and to submerge my conscience into a safer place, free of anxiety and degrading self-talk. When I entered the library, the soothing and familiar scent of dusty paper smattered with ink tickled my nostrils. My eyes glazed over looking across the rows of darkly polished wood shelves adorned with bound volumes and filled with the abundance of knowledge that I was seeking. In those volumes, I discovered that I loved science, specifically biology. And of course learning anything about animals was also at the top of that list.

As winter gripped the prairies of Alberta in its frozen grasp, we were forced indoors. This meant keeping busy to avoid the distasteful stares from my mother and spending a lot of time in my room. My inquisitive mind was fascinated by the cycle of life and death and all of the stages in between. I'd perform experiments in my bedroom with Paul as my trusted assistant. I wanted to know how fast under controlled and uncontrolled conditions that chicken, fish, beef, and pork would grow maggots and produce adult flies. Odd thought process perhaps but inquiring minds wanted to know.

On separate occasions I set up three jars; all three containing a small piece of raw protein. I left the first jar open, uncontrolled. I put mesh over the top of jar number two and sealed it with an elastic; and jar number three I sealed without any airflow. I placed them on the floor in the corner of my room and watched them closely for changes. I wrote lengthy documents daily detailing the results in a journal where I could express myself freely. I enjoyed writing and daydreamed that one day I'd be recognized for my data findings. Things like that don't happen to kids like me because during our next move I lost my recorded data as once again my life was bounced from the back of a truck and strewn across the highway.

I saw the familiar signs of a change coming quickly in the early spring when our pets started disappearing at an alarming rate without any explanation. I was a farm girl, and I knew that some animals were food because I'd grown up hunting, skinning, and butchering them to survive. I wasn't blind to where meat and poultry came from; however, in my eyes there is a difference between food and pet and I was unaware that some of my pets were in fact edible.

Have you ever heard the saying: *running around like a chicken with its head cut off*? Well, it's a real thing. Paul and I were torn on more than one occasion as we watched in disgust but laughed hysterically as a chicken would flap its wings and frantically run around the barnyard spraying blood from the place where its head once was. When it ran out of steam and flopped over dead we'd cut off its feet and chase each other as we pulled on the slimy tendons running up the back to make them grasp and grip the air between us. As gross as it may have been, the laughter he and I shared was worth every gag in my throat.

One day in spring Paul and I were occupying our time playing and jumping around in the yard with our few remaining pet goats. I loved the goats because they were clumsy and playful and made me laugh, but my father liked them because they also produced milk like cows.

While we were running and laughing I looked up and noticed a truck pulling into the yard. I couldn't see inside and didn't recognize the truck so we stayed where we were and watched. My father approached the vehicle, spoke briefly to the driver, and pointed the truck in the direction of the barn.

Once parked the door opened and three of the skinniest, tallest, and blackest men I had ever seen stepped out into the yard, speaking to my father in broken English.

Paul and I went about our business and back to our fun at hand. But soon there was a familiar, high-pitched whistle from across the yard that my father used to summon us, and we ran over to see what he wanted. To our confusion we were told that the goats now belonged to these men and were instructed to gather them up with ropes and bring them to the barn. I was heartbroken because these were the last of the pets we had left, and I was being made to give them away.

Paul and I did as we were told sadly and as slowly as we could to lengthen the time we had left with them. I collected the bigger two and Paul roped the smaller, feisty one that was our favorite, and we made our way back to the barn with tears streaming down our dirty faces. My father told Paul to hand the goat to the older of the men and he did. The next moments happened so fast that there wasn't even time to process it. One man grabbed my small goat by her hind legs and held her upside down. Another man produced a machete and as my pet hung there bleating her displeasure; he skillfully slit her throat, silencing her.

I watched in horror and disbelief as they effortlessly strung her up in the barn to bleed out. Her blood dripped into a pool beneath her and mixed with the dirt; the metallic smell of blood that I knew well permeated the air. As the man started walking towards the goats that I was holding, I had the desperate urge to run, but instead I dropped the ties and gathered Paul into my arms. I ran into the house where we didn't have to witness any more of our loved ones die at the hands of strangers.

My relationship with my father deteriorated after this incident; I couldn't believe he could be so cruel. But he was. He was just like everyone else.

There was talk of some financial complications at the shop resulting in the trike being taken, and I was told we were moving. Again. I'd formed friendships in that short time, didn't want to leave, and returned to being sullen. In April of 1983 when I was fifteen years old, we embarked on move number eleven, this time to Quesnel, British Columbia.

A Bumpy Start to the Morning

Moving to Quesnel had its perks although from an angry teen's perspective they were few and far between. We were still out in the country, which was welcomed, but in a community meaning no pets other than a dog or two. My mother's sister, Aunt Viv, and her son Shawn lived there right across the back fence. I'd met them and a couple of other relatives over the years but didn't have relationships with them other than talking over the phone. I remember a few conversations with my Aunt Lily in California who sounded like she was singing when she spoke because she was always so happy, and I liked that.

I enjoyed getting to know and spending time with my relatives. My cousin Shawn and I were exactly the same age right down to the date. We often joked about who was older, and in my 1984 school yearbook he wrote: *Roses are red, violets are blue, no matter what you do, I will always be older than you – your loving cousin*. In that very same book my father wrote: *Knockers up*. A perverse reminder of my objectification.

Shawn was the first male I could be alone with and not feel unsafe or intimidated. He was always laughing, friendly, and trying to include me in things he was doing with his friends. I secretly wondered what my life would've been like if he were my brother.

Ryan was out of sight but not out of mind while Shawn was present and nice to me. The uniquely shared birthday that we celebrated and our love of music bonded us together over time as more than cousins. We became treasured friends. We'd sit in his room for hours on end while he played his favorite songs on his cassette tape deck like a DJ. We could feel the bass bouncing off the walls, and I'd close my eyes and get lost in the music, singing the songs in my head. I'd reminisce about my special day of singing with Carrie and wish I possessed the courage to sing out loud again.

I wasn't confident enough for that, and I'd been taught to be seen and not heard my entire life. I developed a spiritual connection to music of all genres and had a knack for listening to a song and retaining the lyrics very quickly. The stronger my need to express what was being said, the quicker I learned it and thankfully I'd passed that love of music on to Paul.

I was proud of him for being such a loving and independent boy whose infectious smile lit up every room he entered. He was an energetic six-year-old who was going to kindergarten fulltime and associating with other children his age. This was new for him because for the better part of his life I was his only lifeline. He was such a joy to be around that most people fell in line to be his friend. I'd never treated him any way other than how I thought a child should be treated even though I never was myself. Something inside of me instinctively knew what was right in spite of how I'd lived. Paul had a slight speech impediment and limp but was he was a healthy, active, adorable, normal little boy.

Although my cousin and everyone else my age was in grade ten, I attended the second round of grade eight that year. Much to my amazement, I was able to pass the year despite being the awkward, new girl. I was a troubled child on the inside, a grown woman on the outside, and trying to be social and fit in with my peers somewhere in between. I'd gained more of an appreciation for school now thanks to the girls and teachers in Calmar. I had a pretty uncomplicated existence because my parents were living their lives and staying out of mine, and Paul was growing up fast. I was meeting new people, making some friends, and casually dating boys. It helped my social life that my cousin introduced me to his friends while I also risked branching out on my own. It didn't take long, and I was surrounded by friends and peers who didn't care where I'd come from and accepted me for who I presented myself as.

I was hopeful every time we moved that something inside of my mother's thick skull would click into place and she would stop hating me. I was more hopeful this time because her sister was within walking distance and posed a new reason to get out of bed. As much as I needed her to succeed as a functioning adult for Paul's sake, it never seemed to happen. For the most part my relationships with my parents were strained at best as I continued to cook, clean, and care of Paul's and my needs.

During the summer months of 1983, my parents were absent a lot. One afternoon they drove to the emergency room in town so my mother could get a shot of Demerol for a migraine episode. These spells were appearing on a weekly basis, sometimes daily basis.

Paul asked if he could go to his friend's house at the end of the block so I walked him there. When we arrived we were shown an old motorized go-cart they'd be playing with. It wasn't working but the chain and sprocket were intact, which allowed for movement by boy-force instead of horse-power. I watched for a few moments as the boys took turns in the driver's seat while the other pushed it forward up and down the straight stretch of road. They were having a great time being boys together so I went home.

I was enjoying some music and my solitude while lying outside on the back deck soaking up some sun when I received a phone call from his friend's grandmother.

"You need to come get Paul right away. He's scratched himself on the go-cart."

I ran like a mother bear on high alert down the street to make sure that my cub was safe and unharmed. When I arrived he had a paper towel draped over his finger and blood was freely running down his arm. This was more than a scratch. I gagged and became nauseous at the sight. I didn't like blood at the best of times, especially not when it's coming out of someone that I love. I put on my maternal hat, swallowed my fear and lifted the paper towel. My stomach lurched and I thought I was going to throw up. I wiped away the blood and looked down at his finger. The end was completely missing and I could see bone.

Even though in a panic, I tried to appear calm. "What happened to your finger?"

He looked at me with trembling lips and blue eyes brimming with tears. "Dusty ate it!" He burst into a fresh bout of tears.

As I consoled Paul his friend told me, "His finger got stuck in the chain and was pinched off and fell to the ground.

Dusty was an Alaskan husky that lived in the neighborhood. He'd been running and playing with the boys when I left. I can only assume that when the digit dropped to the ground all he saw was a warm treat that required gobbling up.

I laughed and cried at the same time as I walked Paul home. My parents arrived at the same time we did. I explained to them what happened and Paul was taken to the hospital to stitch up the end of his finger. There was no getting it back.

We lived near the top of a tall, winding, tree covered hill. The small town and our school were all the way at the bottom. Every school day I'd get Paul and myself ready and we'd catch the bus on the main road. We'd sit at the back of the bus on the weathered and cracked bench seats and wait in anticipation. When we hit a bump on the road the back of the bus would kick up violently and rocket our bodies into the air, smashing us into the roof before we dropped back onto our seats. The bus erupted in a roar of laughter each and every time and it was a memorable and fun way to start the mornings.

I was going to school on a fairly regular basis to be a positive role model for Paul and was making more friends than ever in my life. Although I enjoyed school for the most part, I continued having difficulties focusing and learning. Other than a couple of classes that I enjoyed, I decided I wasn't there to learn anyhow. I was far more interested in the social activities that I'd never known before.

I was an active and eager participant in home economics, drama, and choir and was proficient in all of them because they were skills that I utilized every day. In home ec. I learned how to use a sewing machine and bake. I already knew how to do these because I'd been watching my father sew clothes for me for years, and I was raising and feeding Paul. In drama I learned how to put on masks to hide who I was and let's face it I was more than proficient at that.

In choir the first song we were taught was "The Sound of Silence" by Simon and Garfunkel and it paradoxically freed my voice the way Carrie had taught me to. I sang aloud with encouragement and enthusiasm, which made my heart sing louder than my voice.

The lyrics were hauntingly familiar, and my throat would constrict with emotion as I'd sing:

Hear my words that I might teach you.

Take my arms that I might reach you.

But my words like silent raindrops fell.

And echoed in the wells of silence.

I knew this feeling all too well.

Because of the long overdue positive contributions in my life, I allowed myself to let my guard down bit by bit. I became more socially aware and slowly blossomed into a young girl who thrived off the happiness of other people and joined in with that feeling. What I came to appreciate about small towns and country schools was that there weren't small groups of people snickering and pointing at each other; everyone was friendly for the most part. Prior to Quesnel I'd been rather quiet, shy, and awkward but after moving there I found a happier sense of being.

I was still a smoker, mind you, and when I wasn't in class, I spent all of my time with my new girlfriends in the "smoke hole" behind school, an area the teachers had designated to the smokers. It kept the mess and smell all in one place and away from those who didn't smoke. The rules were simple and few: do not step onto the sidewalk even with the slightest edge of your shoe or you'd be sent to the principal's office, and huddle close together when it is cold outside, which in the mountains of British Columbia is eight months out of the year.

I learned how to be a popular teenage girl in the confines of that sidewalk lined rectangle. I was regularly hanging out with different groups of girls, each instrumental in helping me learn to relax and become more outgoing. Life was better than I ever imagined it could be. I was hanging out at girlfriends' houses, going to parties, and living the life of an average, Canadian teen. Every weekend I could be found riding shotgun in a car with the bass pumping hard with a gaggle of girls singing "Girl's Night Out" by the band Toronto at the top of our lungs.

The year rolled by and it was soon January 1984 and my birthday. I was excited to turn sixteen because for the first time in my life there were many blue sky days, and I had hope of a sunshiny future. I surprisingly received three presents from my parents that year, which was unusual. My mother gave me a magnum of Baby Duck wine, which was my favorite and helped me accept the gifts I was about to receive from my father.

He offered me two possessions and a lesson that I'll remember for the rest of my days. The first was a delicate gold ring with a very small diamond chip on it, essentially a gold wire with a slight setting. I thought it was beautiful and although it was small in size, the sentiment more than made up for it. The second was a full length, sheer, pale green night gown.

He was adamant I model it for him right away, which I begrudgingly did. I went into my bedroom to put it on and came out wearing a bra and panties underneath because it was see-through. He didn't like this and told me that type of night gown wasn't worn with underwear and sent me back to my room to remove them. I did what I was told because he said so.

Later that evening, my mother and father were sitting on the couch watching TV while I sat uncomfortably wearing my new see-through night gown and diamond ring, getting buzzed on Baby Duck wine. I must have either fallen asleep or passed out on the floor because the next thing I knew I felt lots of weight on top of me. I lay there paralyzed and confused. Ryan wasn't around but the familiar smell of fear, cigarettes, and beer enveloped me. I opened my eyes to see what was happening as his beard grazed my ear and face and he pressed his body into mine.

He groaned deeply and whispered, "I love you; you're so beautiful. No one will be as gentle with you as I will be. I've waited long enough."

His erection strained against the flimsy shelter of my silk. I clasped my legs together tightly.

"Please," I begged, "get off of me."

He climaxed immediately and his body convulsed against mine, leaving his excitement on my new night gown. He rolled over quickly and pulled up his pants. He nonchalantly strode away like nothing had happened and went to go sleep next to my mother.

As with my other abuses, I was alone; I couldn't tell anyone my dirty secrets out of shame. I pushed and tucked them deep inside where only I knew they were. I was smoking pot regularly again and my alcohol consumption escalated to numb me through the days. My father was drying the Mary Jane in the large window at the front room of the house, so it's not like it was a secret that we had the shit.

I stopped going to school regularly and shifted back to an angrier, more closed off girl. I pushed away friends and started staying out all night and partying hard at bush parties, often getting so hammered that I'd black out. I was lost, alone, and had dug myself back into the dark and lonely hole I'd barely just succeeded in climbing out of.

When my *who gives a fuck?* attitude returned, oddly enough so did my objectification through photo sessions with my father. Because I was disgusted with him, you would think it would have been the opposite, right? I should have avoided him like the plague, but I didn't and our relationship became different—strained, but still there. He was the only functioning parent I knew and although he tried to hurt me, I believed he hadn't succeeded.

In an effort to thwart off any more advances from my father seeking my virginity, I consensually gave it away to a boy I was dating at the time. We went to a party, and I was drunk or high, probably both, and had sex in his best friend's bed while the party raged on upstairs. I didn't care; it beat my other alternative.

The next day I felt a great sense of relief and utter embarrassment when my boyfriend confirmed for me that I was a virgin. His friend had bitched at him because there was blood all over his sheets. Not the greatest news to hear that I soiled someone's bed, but at least I knew for sure that no one else had taken it. I was thankful that I'd given my virginity to someone I shared feelings with, even if it was under duress, instead of having it taken against my will.

The incident with my father put a bad taste in my mouth, and gave me a fresh anger to release, which I had no problem doing. There was one girl who was taunting me about my *retarded little brother* and told me she wasn't afraid of me because I couldn't fight. After school there was an excited group of kids around me waiting for the bus and the pulse of their excitement physically carried me closer to her. We stopped and the kids made a circle around her and me, blocking any chance of escape. I pinned her to the side of the bus and wrapped my hands around her throat like a constrictor on its prey. I stood there choking her as I'd been choked in the past.

I could hear the kids behind me cheering and taunting me to *punch her, punch her, punch her!* I didn't want to hurt anyone, I just wanted to scare her and let her know that I was watching and listening. I squeezed her throat tighter for a second to punctuate my point and my knuckles grew white.

Mother bear was in protection mode when I looked deep into her eyes and whispered, "Never talk bad about Paul again, or next time I won't be as nice."

I released my hold and allowed her to breathe as I walked away. She didn't speak Paul's name again and never so much as looked in my direction.

I may have physically gone to the school, but I wasn't really there for classes. During one of my brief appearances at school I met another girl named Debbie, and the instant connection I felt to her was undeniable. She was a deep thinker who wrote beautiful poetry that inspired me and she encouraged me to write my thoughts down as well. There were no rules to follow and writing became my private outlet of expression that I freely allowed her to read.

She was quiet like me around the other girls but comfortably snorted when she laughed when she was with me. We snorted together without shame. I could be myself around her and feel comfortable in my weirdness. She just got me. We clicked, and she was exactly who I needed in my life.

If I could have had a sister, she would have been it. We bonded as spiritual sisters-from-other-misters through raucous laughter, music, poetry, eating poutine, and video games at the arcade. Having her friendship and love balanced out the anguish and torment I was feeling.

The kids at school thought it would be cute to call Debbie and me *The Debsi Twins*. I was Debsi One because I was older and she was Debsi Two. To ensure the nicknames were never forgotten and to add some hilarity to our lives, Two constructed us matching pins to wear. They were four-inch circles of bright yellow construction paper with *Debsi Twins Rule* written in black lettering. We displayed them proudly on our chests so everyone knew and no one would mistake who was who.

In the summer of 1984, my Two and I spent our days hanging out with Paul, who was seven, and our nights partying hard. She was living with us because she was fiery-spirited like me, and her parents were quite restrictive, which led her to rebelling. Our parents mutually agreed to let her stay at our house to stop the fighting in theirs. What better place for her to unwind than a place with zero restrictions? My house didn't have rules. She could do what she wanted, when she wanted, with whomever she wanted—no questions asked—and I was beside myself to have company. She distracted me from the hateful glares that I received from my mother and helped me with Paul. I'd never had voluntary help before with anything, and it solidified my sisterly love for her.

Long, lazy days of summer turned to fall and school began again, much to my chagrin. I'd miraculously made it to grade nine and was living what I thought was a typical teenage life. Friendships and relationships were made. Others were ended. School remained a challenge to attend, but I made the best of it with my Two beside me.

Grief on the Cold, Hard, Freshly-Turned Dirt

When I turned seventeen years old in January 1985, life once again took a turn for the worse. My parents told me that Ryan was moving in right away, and that I was allowed to have a party for my birthday—all in the same breath.

I stood in disbelief. I hadn't thought of my brother for quite some time but there I was gripped in the familiar fear he conjured. But I wasn't alone this time though; I had a protector with Debsi Two by my side.

I avoided him at all costs after he moved in. It wasn't that hard to do because he got a job and quickly met people, which kept him away from the house. He was partying harder than I was, and I already knew from experience what that did to him, so the less he was around the happier I was.

Having a party for my birthday was a pretty shitty consolation prize in light of their other news but better than nothing. I was hanging out with a few new people and had developed a crush on a boy named Lyle. I considered him to be one of my closest guy friends but was scared to expose my secret feelings. I didn't want to ruin the friendship or make it awkward. I invited him and some other friends over as well. But I planned to tell him how I felt. I'd dated other boys in town but only had a sexual encounter with the one and wasn't quite ready to do that again. But I wanted him to know I liked him.

The date for my party was set for the following weekend, and all I had to do was wait nervously. Lyle had gotten his driver's license a few days before and told me that he was excited to come to my place because his parents were allowing him to drive there.

A couple of days before my party, I received a phone call from a mutual friend of ours from school. He sounded choked up, and I could barely hear him.

"Are you okay?" I asked. "What's wrong?'

He managed to say, "I got a call from Lyle's sister. There was an accident. Lyle's dead."

Was this some kind of cruel joke? My throat tightened and as his words rushed through my veins and reached my heart, it ached. A deep and numbing that I hadn't felt since the passing of my childhood friend Carrie. I couldn't use my heart. I needed to use my head and survival mode presented itself.

With tears slowly rolling down my cheeks I whispered, "What happened?"

He explained that Lyle and a couple of his buddies were practicing driving up and down a hill when it began to snow. He accelerated around a corner and the truck hydroplaned over a puddle, flipped, rolled, and mangled the vehicle and the driver.

The rest of the conversation and days that followed were a blur. My party was cancelled. There was nothing left to celebrate.

The day of his funeral was one of mourning for the whole community, and we all came together to grieve the loss of his young life. As a supportive group, we piled into the back of a couple of trucks and made our way to his grave site. I sat there, like everyone else, emotionless, numb, and empty at such a tragic loss. I didn't even really react physically until I saw them lower his casket into the ground. I found myself consumed with the overwhelming desire to go into that hole with him, and without even thinking I threw myself onto the cold, hard, freshly turned dirt and cried like I'd never cried before. Tears of past emotional pain, frustration, and loss poured out of me uncontrollably and soaked into the dry soil. I didn't care that everyone there was watching as I filled his grave with my sorrow and tears. I grieved not only for him, but for every loved one I'd ever lost, including myself. I was lost and not sure how to heal my own years of pain.

A week after the funeral as I continued to process and move on from my grief, a friend stopped by the house to pay me a visit. It was one of the boys who was in the accident with Lyle. When he arrived, I opened the door, and he silently handed me a prettily wrapped present. I was confused.

He explained that it was a birthday present from Lyle. He'd purchased and wrapped it just before the accident. Lyle was going to give it to me at my party, and his friend thought I should have it.

I cried a fresh batch of tears at his gesture of kindness from beyond the grave. That night before I went to sleep I thanked Lyle for showing me that he cared about me and promised I would never forget him. He'd always be with me.

I hadn't received a lot of presents in my life that didn't come attached with a painful memory but this wasn't like that. This was a gift of friendship and love and was the most precious so far. It was a tall, pink, bubbly shaped container of bubble bath that I used sparingly over many years to prolong the use.

It wasn't long after this when my Two moved back home to resolve the differences with her parents, and they moved her to away to start a new life. I was heartbroken.

Other than Paul's love, my world was lifeless and bleak. I was alone and grieving with far too many responsibilities in taking care of Paul and the house. School just wasn't a priority for me anymore, and I quit.

The Trunk of Secrets and a White Suitcase

In 1986 after my eighteenth birthday I was legally considered an adult even though I had been playing the role for many years. My parents sat me down and told me they were moving back to Edmonton and asked if I wanted to go with them or not. We'd been living in Quesnel for just over three years, which was longer than any other place in my life. I wasn't sure I wanted to leave just yet.

I had family and a few friends remaining who I hadn't fully pushed away. My relationships with my parents remained strained at best, but they were the only family I knew, so I was torn. In all honesty, I think the only reasons I decided to move back to Edmonton were because I couldn't leave Paul alone with my parents, and it dawned on me that legal drinking age in Alberta was eighteen; the idea of being able to do it legally was very appealing to me.

Within a few weeks of our conversation, we packed up and headed back to the prairies of Alberta where we saddled up in residence number twelve. Thankfully, Ryan decided to stay in Quesnel and continue to fuck up his life from there, and I could continue to avoid him from a distance.

My relationship with my father was awkward and strained but still functioning. He was my father, and I knew no other and accepted life with him for what it was. I wasn't a flashy girl who wore pretty dresses and make-up but preferred a natural look while wearing jeans, T-shirts, and sneakers because I didn't like bringing attention to myself. Attention caused pain, and I avoided it as much as possible, and after Lyle's death I reverted back to my solitary, introverted self.

The first night we settled into our new condo, my father suggested that he and I go out for my first legal drink together. Although I'd been illegally drinking regularly for almost a decade I was interested in seeing what the inside of a bar looked like, and I willingly agreed.

He clearly anticipated me agreeing because he instructed me to curl my hair, put on some make-up, and handed me a tiny bundle of clothing. He smiled lecherously at me and told me he wanted me to look like a woman, not a little girl, on my big night out. Inside the bundle was a small, red, sequined tank top, a black micro-mini skirt that I thought was a tube top, and some very high black heels to wear.

I looked at him like he was nuts and reminded him it was the middle of winter and this wasn't enough to keep me warm. He brushed away my reasoning, told me we'd be inside, and ushered me into my room to change. I obediently did what I was told.

I transformed myself into who he wanted and walked over to scrutinize my reflection in the mirror. I scanned myself up and down, looking for imperfections that he was sure to point out. I knew I must look picture perfect. He was right though, putting those clothes on did make me look the way he had intended. I looked like a woman.

I uncomfortably placed my 5'2", 123 pound, well-stacked body on display in exchange for my father's desired affection. I possessed all the right bumps in all the right places to lure a man's eye; however, my own eyes reflected a self-conscious girl doing what she was told because she knew no better. If I did what I was told, my father would love me.

I cautiously expressed discomfort about my lack of clothing, and he told me, "You look fuckin' hot; don't worry about it. After a couple of drinks, it won't matter."

We went to a dimly light lounge that was in a hotel lobby. There was loud music pumping out of large, black speakers hidden in the corners and cigarette smoke danced on the air in time with the music. I was intoxicated by the atmosphere and started to relax about my appearance.

I wasn't sure how to sit, stand, dance, or even breathe in the skimpy outfit I was wearing, but I smiled through it. I'd been faking and hiding my feelings for eighteen years and this scenario was no different for me, simply an adaptation. Whisky helped.

My father was an aggressive man when sober but when the whisky hit his veins he became louder and more physically demanding in his mannerisms towards me, like on my sixteenth birthday. His true personality emerged when intoxicated and his actions were more like a boyfriend, and I was his piece of ass, not his daughter.

I tried to have fun as I sang loudly and we danced a couple of times to bass-filled rock songs as alcohol became his excuse. He was in its grasp, and he wanted to slow dance with me; I did not want to. That didn't matter though because I wasn't in a position to tell him no and even if I was, he wouldn't have heard it.

Visions of my sixteenth birthday flashed behind my closed eyes as he nuzzled his beard into my neck whispering, "You're a sexy little cock tease," as he swayed against me.

I did nothing to stop him; I just followed along hoping it would soon be over like on that fateful night not so long before.

When we sat down a man at the next table us asked me, "Are you okay honey?"

I responded quickly with a nod and a smile.

I knew not to speak with other men in my father's presence. But he'd seen the exchange, igniting his possessive jealousy. A few cooed words of my cajoling lightened his mood somewhat. He wanted to dance again and dragged me onto the dance floor to succumb to another slow song. He wrapped his scrawny arms around me, his body snaking against mine, and tried to kiss me on the mouth. He grabbed the back of my arms and pulled me into him. I turned my head slowly so his lips only grazed the side of my mouth and tried not to look disgusted. Over my shoulder the other man was watching us intently as he and my father competed in a stare down.

The men were probably looking at us because we were the oddest and most unlikely looking couple in the place. My father was a skinny, grease-stained, biker who resembled Willie Nelson mixed with John Lennon, and I was an impish girl wearing as little clothing as possible without being naked, or arrested, while balancing in five-and-a-half-inch stilettos.

When the man who had asked if I was all right confronted my father, a verbal altercation ensued. This escalated into a physical one and resulted in us being kicked out and banned for life from the premises. My father drove us home three-sheets-to-the-wind drunk, and that was the first and last I drank with my father outside of our house.

Attempting to temporarily escape the insanity I was living in, I contacted a couple of people I'd known previously. We met up and partied together, which introduced me to new people. While out one night I met a ray of sunshine who would become my new best friend and partner in crime. Her name was Lavern. We liked each other right off the bat and were soon spending every waking moment together. She was oh-so-girly and taught me how to style my hair, put on make-up, and walk and dance in heels.

I was fascinated by the amount of clothing and shoes she owned, and it just so happened we were exactly the same size. She wore tight, little, colorful 80s spandex dresses that hugged and accentuated every bump and curve of the body, and then I dressed the same way. The events of my life transformed a small town, party girl into a grown woman living in the big city where getting wasted was legal, and there were many places to do it.

My parents moving me back to Alberta was not one of their most bright and shining moments, but it was the perfect place for me to escalate my self-destruction to a whole other level, and I had company! Beautiful, sun-shiny company and you know what they say about misery!

One day Lavern and I were hanging out at my house when my father suggested that I show her the special sit-ups I could do. He taught me how to do them when I was younger, and I didn't think they were unusual and did them with him on a regular basis. I did as I was told and began showing her the exercises he was talking about. As I started my routine I could see a sour expression on her face. I stopped what I was doing, and we went into my room to listen to music. I asked about the look she'd given me. Lavern said she thought it was weird that I did them like that with my father, which left me confused, but I didn't push the subject any further.

Isn't it normal for a father to encourage his young daughter to be healthy and to exercise and perform special sit-ups that were twice as hard as regular sit-ups? Isn't it normal for a young girl to jump on her father's torso and wrap her legs tightly around him only to lean backwards and touch her head to his knees while being encouraged to do more, and more, and more? Often times I could feel him get hard underneath me which was when my exercise lesson would end for me, and I would disengage as it made me uncomfortable. This was normal to me.

I didn't hold affection for the male species really other than Paul and my cousin Shawn and the oddly obligatory affection that I felt towards my father. I could only identify that feeling as love. And because I thought I loved him, I would do almost anything for him.

My father had always been touchy-feely with me so when that behavior became even more so when my mother wasn't around, it seemed normal. My mother didn't notice or pretended not to. She was close to her favorite amenities again and quickly returned to her life of men, pills, and injections while I ran her household. I can honestly say that I saw her in a horizontal position more often than an upright one—unless she was angry, then she could move quite quickly. I was used to her absence and preferred it when she wasn't around because our relationship had always been unhealthy and toxic. She claimed no use for me, and I'd lost hope in receiving affection from her as well, so no love was lost.

The only thing I asked of her was to make sure that Paul was taken care of when I wasn't there. He was a healthy, active, nine-year-old boy who went to school every day and walked, ran, or rode his bike wherever he went and loved me to pieces. There would be hell to pay from this mother bear if she didn't protect him.

Although I was drinking and smoking pot regularly, I was present and accounted for in Paul's life. I made it my mission to make sure that he received all the things he needed and deserved every day as I continued to be his only maternal role. He was my adorable little brother, and I couldn't imagine my life without his smile brightening up my very dark world on a daily basis.

I thought my face was plain-Jane and nondescript other than an unusually large dimple that I possess on my right cheek. When I put the effort into my hair, make-up, and wearing more provocative clothing, I felt better about myself. I definitely got more attention. I felt more confident after I was taught how to disguise the sadness that lurked in my green eyes with a few coats of mascara and this development caught the attention of you know who. My father took this as an open invitation to escalate his picture taking to an all-time high.

He also encouraged my use of intoxicants. I was less bitchy and more playful when I was intoxicated, so he kept me that way in his company. He would supply me with whatever I needed for our photo sessions; a hoot or a shot, most times a couple of each. Verbal objectification was a regular occurrence. I was bits and pieces not a whole, and the boys were gonna love me because of my hot little body. I wanted to be loved so I showed my assets.

He set up a makeshift studio in the basement for privacy. In it was a large wicker chair which was a favorite prop of his and his *trunk of secrets*.

I'd seen and posed on the trunk many times throughout my life. It was always locked and I never bothered to give it a second glance until now because it was in front of me and open. My father was upstairs answering the phone so I quickly moved over to see what was inside. It was filled with the numerous costumes of barely-there undergarments, sheer lingerie, and heels in every color of the rainbow that he provided for my pictures.

There was something else familiar about them, but I couldn't put my finger on it. I quickly rummaged through the trunk and my fingers grazed something near the bottom. I reached in to retrieve the item I'd touched, and couldn't believe my eyes. It was the white suitcase that I'd found when I was eleven during a family vacation. I'd blocked it out.

I opened it to confirm the contents and the albums and photos remained. I blanched and closed it. I shoved it back to the bottom and jumped across the room to wait for his return.

My mind raced a million miles a second. How could I have forgotten the white suitcase? Fuck that, how was I going to act normal when he returned? I closed my eyes and concentrated on my breathing to slow my heart rate down just as he came back down the stairs. I excused myself for a bathroom break because I needed a few moments to myself. I was nothing more to him than the images in his photos. An object to use and toss into a ratty old suitcase. I was sex and the woman he'd groomed me to be.

I looked hard at myself in the bathroom mirror and my reflection was blank. I noticed a tiny red dot on my chest and I scratched and picked at it mindlessly while processing my thoughts and feelings, which resulted in a bigger red dot. I didn't care. I was an object, not beautiful, and any thought of a blue sky dream was replaced with purple sky realities. When I went back downstairs I couldn't make eye contact with him. I went and sat where I knew I was expected to.

Before my ass hit the seat he stood over me, his face screwed up disapprovingly. "What the fuck? Why is your chest all red?"

Tears stung my eyes. I lied and quietly said, "I'm sorry. I was itchy and scratched it." Lying didn't come easy to me.

His expression was a mix of anger and disappointment, so I apologized meekly for ruining his plans but was secretly relieved it was over. I was a spirited soul, but when my father spoke my soul clammed up and I listened; everyone listened.

He ordered, "Get out of my sight!"

I ran to my room where I let the tears continue to flow as my thoughts were tormented by long forgotten images.

In the days that followed I'd strategically pinch and break the skin on my face and upper chest with my finger nails causing sores, scabs. These flaws had stopped him the first time, and I wanted to physically dissuade him from taking pictures of me. My self-mutilating scheme didn't continue for long because he covered my imperfections with makeup and did what he wanted. My opinion didn't matter, and I'd inflicted enough damage to create scars outside to match the ones inside, so I stopped.

I wish I could confess that I was the only girl who my father harassed or flirted with into posing for pictures but that would be a lie. I can uncomfortably report that throughout my life, 95 percent of my female friends allowed their pictures to be taken by him... provocative pictures. I don't recall anyone telling him no because he was just that convincing and manipulative that children just fell under his spell. He was everyone's favorite Uncle and family friend.

They agreed to pose, but they also agreed my father was creepy and they wouldn't have felt safe at our house without me in it. I didn't feel safe with me there; I'm not sure how they could. While at our house my friends never left my side, and we'd literally use the bathroom together. I didn't care; I was taught no inhibitions.

Paul was a friendly and gentle ten-year-old boy who attending school regularly, made friends easily, and loved singing while cleaning or cooking dinner with me. His angelic voice and innocent joy was infectious. I mattered to him, and I was doing something right despite living a dual life. There were days when I felt I was slowly losing control but held on for his sake because he needed me just as much as I needed him.

After I rediscovered the suitcase, I decided I needed to move away from my father if I wanted to save myself. He became more aggressive in touching me and vocalizing his desire for pictures, but I wasn't interested and made excuses to squirm away and decline. I saw him in a different light now. His touch and presence repulsed me, and I wished he wasn't my father.

With a glimmer of hope for a new start I found a job working at a clothing store. I started to save up a few dollars and within a couple of months I'd put away a pretty good chunk of change and started to plan my escape. Now, trust me when I say that this was an extremely hard decision for me to make. I knew I couldn't stay under a roof with my parents any longer, and I couldn't take Paul with me either. My heart and my brain battled loudly because I knew when I moved I'd have to leave Paul to take care of himself.

He and I were closer than siblings because I'd mothered him for eight years, and all we had was each other. He was a smart and funny boy who was unknowingly trapped under a purple sky that I pretended to keep blue every day while mine was a very stark landscape of raging storms. Heartbroken, I decided that I needed to be selfish and take my own safety into consideration and chose to make the move. I sat Paul down and discussed my plans with him because I knew how abandonment felt, and I didn't want him to experience that. He was upset I was leaving but excited knowing he could help me move and visit my new place for sleepovers.

I reasoned with myself that I'd move close to my parent's house so I could visit Paul on a regular basis to check on his care. I harbored hope that my mother would leave her bedroom in my absence, but I'd taught him how to cook and take care of himself just in case. My parents were inadequate but not dangerous unless you had lips, tits, and ass, and Paul wasn't defined by any of those.

Within a week, I packed up my few belongings and moved into residence number thirteen with a girl I'd met at work. I was free to express myself.

I dyed my naturally dirty blonde hair to a shocking platinum and smeared on jet black eyeliner and lipstick to distract and obscure the girl I thought I was. I stopped wearing brightly colored, feminine clothing and opted for mostly black, tight, and extremely revealing attire that drew attention to the only features that mattered. I transformed my exterior from a fresh, natural glow to one that reflected the dark torment I felt inside.

I stopped partying with cheerful and energetic Lavern at the bubblegum dance bars and started frequenting a hard rock-punk bar with my roommate. I could be pissed off and pretend not to give a fuck there. We danced wildly and elicited wanted attention while a heavy metal band performed on stage. I was starving and drank up the attention I was getting. It was almost as intoxicating as what was in my glass, if not more. We were partying on tour busses and flirting with band members who were rolling through town for that week. I learned quickly that the girls with the band always got free drinks, and who doesn't like free drinks? I had a high tolerance for alcohol because I'd been an alcoholic for almost a decade already, and people were shocked at how much I could drink and still function. Was I functioning though?

I looked and flirted like the experienced woman I was taught to be, but in reality I'd still only had intercourse once. The thought of doing it again scared the shit out of me, but I knew eventually it would be inevitable. It was nowhere near the top of my list of things to do, but I hoped when it did happen again it would be by choice.

My roommate was a sweet and innocent girl when I met her, just as I appeared a few short months ago. I helped transform her look too. I wanted someone to feel as fucked up as I did to make it seem normal and tried to take her down that road with me. Thankfully she put up one hell of a fight, and I didn't succeed. But that meant a few months later she'd tolerated enough of my 24/7 partying and kicked me out with no notice.

I was self-medicating with alcohol, pot, and hash to alleviate my inner turmoil but wasn't interested in chemicals or anything I'd have to eat, snort, or heaven forbid inject into my veins. Some say that marijuana is a gateway drug, but I don't agree. In my experience it was a harmless, natural plant that grew in the ground and had medicinal healing properties— unlike tobacco—and I liked it. In the world I was living in hard drugs were frequently dangled under my nose but I never took a bite; I got messed up enough from alcohol, thanks.

My soul was like the suitcase because it housed the secrets and indiscretions of my parents. They were both shoved to the bottom of an inescapable dark trunk that looked innocent enough until closer inspection. I needed someone to look deeper.

I moved back in with my parents because it was available on short notice, and I consciously dialed down my party habits. I was under the same roof as Paul again. I recognized that my addiction to alcohol was a problem and that's not how I wanted him to see me. I needed to take control and make a change in my life, or possibly not have one at all.

From the Frying Pan into the Flame

The healing love and affection from Paul in my life again opened the teeniest-tiniest crack of blue in an ominous purple sky. My mother took care of Paul in my absence but instantly scuttled back into her bedroom when I reentered the house, which meant I was expected to be responsible again.

I quit my day job and found another working graveyard and weekend shifts. I was a nighthawk, and it was the perfect plan to keep me busy during a time when I was usually drinking and partying. I wanted to live a sober life, so I decided I just wouldn't drink.

Ryan wasn't living with us but maintained a relationship with our parents and would visit them from time to time. He was twenty-two years old, married, and living in Ponoka, Alberta, with his new wife. I had hoped he'd have mellowed out with the love of his wife, but that wasn't the case. I could protect myself, but I was still afraid of him and tried to avoid him when he visited, but sometimes that aversion wasn't always possible. Without fail, each time I ran into him there was a higher level of anger, violence, and disregard of precious life demonstrated, and I wanted no part of it.

Shortly after starting my new job at the convenience store, I met a guy named Ron who worked at a gas station across the street from where I was working. I was cautious with men but more confident I could protect myself because I held no fear, as the rapport of our friendship started off innocently enough.

He'd frequent the store on his breaks or before and after his shifts to buy candy or drinks and flirt. When we first met I wasn't attracted to him physically, nor was I interested in dating anyone. He wasn't the type of guy I would've normally been attracted to anyhow. Not that I had a specific type, but he definitely was not it. He was a six-foot-tall rocker with a stocky build and black, waist-length, frizzy, 1980s hair. He was a dark and edgy musician with a hard look about him until he smiled; it was crooked and mischievous.

The first time he asked me out was when we were having a conversation about things we liked to do. I told him, "I love to eat, laugh, and listen to music," to which he jokingly retorted, "We should do those together sometime."

I laughed it off and declined, but that didn't stop him from continuing to come around and ask. I was skeptical of men after a lifetime of being subjected to violence and abuse and was uninterested in him or anyone else romantically. He was persistent however, and slowly over time he grew on me.

I denied him dates but secretly swooned over his pursuits for my attention and the flirtatious banter we engaged in. I didn't want to like him but did and visited him at his job when I wasn't working. I fought it because I didn't want to end up like my parents in a loveless relationship but decided there were no reasons we couldn't be friends—and I was looking for a roommate. He was funny, charming, and made me laugh, which was important to me because laughter was an essential piece in surviving my past.

His persistence paid off and a short time later when he asked, "Do you think we could ever enjoy food, laughter, and music together?" I allowed myself to be happy and said yes to a date. I took a chance.

We began dating and our relationship progressed rapidly. In the beginning he was affectionate and loving towards me, and I felt safe around him. We spent our time together at his place, which was the perfect reprieve for me from my home life. It appeared that life was looking up and about to improve. I liked my new job and new boyfriend; things were going in the right direction.

Within the first month of our whirlwind romance, he proposed to me with his mother's wedding ring. I was over the moon ecstatic and immediately shrieked yes. I was excited to start a life with a man unlike my father who wanted to keep me from harm and be with me forever. We decided that we wanted to live together right away because he'd convinced me that life was going to change for the better. What a fool I had been to resist him in the beginning!

Lavern cheerfully reentered my life and was happy I was settling down because she was too. But just as she had seen clearly my father's behavior was off and inappropriate, she also expressed her distaste for Ron.

The first time she met him she commented, "I don't trust him; he has creepy eyes."

The next time she met him she again expressed her dislike. "He's not the man for you, sweetie. You can do better."

I ignored these warnings. I just wanted to be happy.

He took the liberty of renting us a small, one-bedroom apartment located on the fourth floor, which solidified move number fifteen for me. Initially it seemed perfect and what I needed to escape the chaos that was my life. On our first night living together, I willingly and consensually gave my body to a man for the second time in my life. I was happier than I'd ever been and thought I'd learned that love didn't have to hurt.

While Ron was out the next day Lavern came over and made a third attempt to sway my perception of the man I loved. Her opinion fell on deaf ears.

"I deserve to feel love from someone other than Paul," I angrily yelled at her. "You are *not* going to stop that from happening! and slammed the door in her face as she left.

Unfortunately, she was right not to like him.

I took his attention and moving fast into a relationship as signs that I was treasured and desired, rather than the red flags that Lavern saw. I wish I'd seen them.

After that day Ron's demeanor changed drastically, and I felt like I'd jumped from the frying pan into the flame. The comical and sweet man I'd met disappeared faster than he'd appeared. He became more possessive and more aggressive. After the first time I surrendered my body to him, he no longer seemed interested in me sexually. This made me doubt and question the womanly charms my father always told me I possessed. As the days passed he belittled me to establish his dominant role.

There was a locking mechanism and bars on the inside of the windows. I thought they were to keep other people from coming in until he said, "I put them there to stop you from getting out."

Ron abused and humiliated me as though he'd taken lessons from my mother. I believed I was the problem and that I didn't deserve the happiness I was seeking. I'd sit there motionless and in silence to make him happy. He'd viciously attack me with words I'd been conditioned to believe were true.

"You are unlovable, you are alone, and you don't matter."

I didn't matter.

A month after we moved in together Ron intercepted a call from my father reminding me about an appointment I'd made with the doctor. I'd forgotten that I'd arranged to have my tonsils removed because they continued to be a problem since childhood. In my excitement to start a new life together with Ron it'd slipped my mind, so I hadn't mentioned it. I meekly told him about the surgery and hoped he'd allow me to go. Ron granted me permission to leave the apartment the day of the surgery.

"It'll keep you quiet for a few days. You like to talk too fuckin' much."

I left that day knowing to keep my mouth shut in the presence of others, or there would be repercussions when I returned, and I wasn't taking any chances.

The surgery was successful, and Ron was there to pick me up afterwards with the advisement that I should rest my throat for a few days because it needed to heal. A few days later, my tongue and throat were rather swollen and sore, and I was having trouble swallowing air, let alone food. I'd tried eating but it hurt far too much so I stuck to sucking on ice and popsicles. Even those hurt.

Four days later, I still wasn't able to eat anything solid and developed a stomach ache, a fever, and was belching up the smell of rotten meat. A few hours later my situation worsened, and I started vomiting a cesspool of rancid smelling chunks from both ends of my body onto the floor.

I was naked, exhausted, and disgusted but knew I had to get my mess cleaned up before he got home or there would be more hell to pay. I cleaned it the best I could, and dragged my fevered and shivering body to bed.

When he came home he noticed that I was passed out on the bed but more importantly that his dinner hadn't been made. That was the first time he physically hit me. He smacked me awake and questioned my laziness and lack of respect in his house. Tears welled up in my eyes, but I couldn't talk to explain. No explanation would've been sufficient anyhow. I pulled myself out of bed and mustered up the energy to make him a pot of spaghetti for dinner.

He insisted that I eat. "It will make you feel better." He put a plate of spaghetti down and motioned for me to eat.

The pain felt like what I imagined hot lava would feel like running down my throat. I broke down into a sobbing, choking mess.

He yelled, "Get out of my sight," and I quickly ran back to the only comfort I knew, bed.

The next morning, I was no better. I cried and begged him to take me to the doctor, and he finally agreed. He insisted that the doctor be female.

"I don't want other men touching my property," he seethed. "If I can't have you, no one can."

I knew that my doctor was a man, but I told him what he wanted to hear so he wouldn't change his mind and not let me go. I was in desperate need of help.

As I exited the vehicle at the clinic he warned me, "I'll be waiting in the parking lot. Be quick!"

I sheepishly darted into the office and was placed into an examination room right away. While I waited for the doctor, I reflected on the state my life was in, and my eyes welled up with tears. The severity of my situation and my need to escape festered with the realization that he was waiting for me outside. I didn't want to go back out there.

I shook the tears away. I didn't want anyone to see my moment of weakness, and I knew that in order to continue surviving I had to be strong. I was stronger than this. I grabbed a box of tissue and placed it on my lap to stifle my last sobs and wipe away my tears. I closed my eyes for a moment and felt the depths of my soul become enveloped in darkness.

I opened my eyes to the doctor asking, "Are you alright?" as he lightly touched my face.

I looked at the floor to break eye contact and hide my embarrassment only to notice the box on my lap was empty. The sheets of tissue were shredded into tiny bits and had fallen to the floor and settled around me. I panicked. How long had I been there? Where was Ron?

I heard the click of the office door opening and cowered because I thought it was Ron. It wasn't. My father entered the room, and I couldn't have been happier to see him. He however, did not look happy to see me. The disappointment was written in the lines of his furrowed brow and no words were spoken between us as my doctor explained what had happened to me.

I was fighting an infection and had just experienced some sort of mental breakdown, due to high stress and trauma over the last couple of months. He said I should be placed into a mental health facility where I could get my head checked and straight, and I shouldn't be left alone.

My father had heard enough. He scooped me off the chair, cradled me in his arms, and walked out the door. I didn't know where Ron was, but I could see that he wasn't waiting in the parking lot anymore. My brain was scrambled, and I was confused because even though I was with my father for the first time in what seemed like forever, ironically enough I felt safe.

He decided that I'd move back into their house, and I was in no frame of mind to argue. Besides that, I didn't really have any other option. When we arrived at the house the silence of a long car ride was broken as my father questioned and reprimanded me loudly.

"What the fuck has been going on in that apartment for the last two months? How long have you been addicted to Valium?"

I was dumbfounded by this question because I was a lot of things in this life, but being a pill-popper like my mother wasn't one of them.

He told me that when the doctor initially phoned, he told him that the blood work done before my surgery showed I had high levels of the drug in my system.

That was when it dawned on me. I thought about the tiny nodules of something bitter I'd noticed in my food over the last couple of months but ignored. Ron must have been crushing up the pills and putting it into my food to keep me under his control from the very beginning, and I was so desperate for love that I didn't see it. It suddenly all made sense.

I wasn't simply fighting an infection; I was battling something far greater. I was having withdrawals from a drug that I wasn't aware I was taking, and my body was detoxifying because I couldn't eat anything.

My father decided against the doctor's recommendation of therapy for me, and life carried on like nothing had happened. I was left to work it out on my own. Ron called the house once about my belongings but my father took the call and set up the arrangements to pick them up. Thankfully he never contacted me or resurfaced in my life ever again.

Purple City and a Chance at Freedom

I assumed that living with my parents after the last few months I'd just spent with Ron would've been a walk in the park for me. Truth be known, I was so very wrong. In the few days after I returned home with my now valium-free body, I found that my emotions and paranoia were highly sensitive. I was easily spooked at every turn. I was constantly worried and looking over my shoulder to see if he'd come to take me back.

I was once again caring for Paul on a full-time basis and found him to be my one and only saving grace. Having him with me at that time was exactly the distraction that I needed; I didn't have time to think about myself when I was in his angelic company or concentrating on his well-being. I felt the need to protect him from the truth, so he was unaware of what I'd endured. I smiled through the emotional agony when he was around because it was my burden to bear, and he didn't need to know that his sister was damaged goods.

A week later, my father announced to my mother that he no longer loved her and that he was in love with our landlady. This wasn't a big shock seeing how my parents were the perfect couple. I'd met our landlady a few times and knew that she too was married to someone else and had two small children: a dark-haired, bright-eyed boy and an adorable blonde girl with sparkling blue eyes. Her children were cute and playful and reminded me of a past when Ryan and I were young like them.

The breakup propelled my mother out of her bedroom and sent her sailing over an edge that she'd already been teetering on for quite some time. She was no longer just a little bit crazy; she was certifiable and angry.

A few days later I was surprised by a welcomed and long overdue visit from my Debsi Two. She and I had stayed in sporadic contact over the last two years and I had told her of the life I'd been manipulated into living. My head and heart were in dark places and in need of some sisterly, healing love, protection, and support that she willingly provided. Fueling my own addiction to alcohol and smoking lots of pot helped me too.

For three days she and I partied hard as we danced and laughed ferociously like we were back in high school, and I tried to pretend that Ron never happened while continuing to watch my back. Her laugh and nurturing spirit were infectious and lighter skies were above by the end of her visit, but before she left I wanted to show her a different reality.

On our last night together, I took her to a place called Purple City. It's not a real place, but a place of fantasy and trickery of the eye, with or without being high. I'd experienced it both ways and each was exceptional in their own vision. Edmonton is the capital of Alberta and houses a large legislative building that sits on the top of a sprawling hill and offers a spectacular view. Although it's scenic all the time, Purple City can only be visited at night. When night falls and the sky goes black, the structure is illuminated by large, yellow lights that give it a hauntingly beautiful glow.

To enter this elusive place, we walked over to one of the obscenely bright yellow lights and looked directly into it for a count of thirty so the golden color from the light could be burned into our retinas. When we looked up the entire landscape was glowing completely purple. Probably not the best thing for our eyes, but I showed her my world on that night without even knowing it.

She left the next day as her life called her back to reality but having her there for that short time and sharing that moment healed me a little. I was a bit lovable, if only to two people.

When it came to the affairs and battles of my parents, I tried to keep Paul and myself as uninvolved as possible. Most of the screaming and yelling took place during the day while he was at school, and I was in my room trying to sleep and stay sober; which wasn't going so well. The tension in the house at that time was so thick you could have cut it with a knife, and based on the level of threats and violence that I'd heard between my parents, someone getting cut was definitely a possibility. In fact, I took it upon myself to make sure that no knives were accessible at all during that time.

My bedroom was in the basement of the condo. The last time I had stayed there I'd discovered that the ceiling was false and that I could hide shit in there. Initially I used the hiding space for my pot, paraphernalia, and alcohol just in case my brother came over. I'd caught him rooting like a pig around my room a few times looking for my stash, but I was smarter than he was; he just didn't know it.

This time I was using that space to hide my father's handgun, bullet magazines, and any sharp knives or objects that could be used as a weapon. I was trying to prevent my parents from killing each other with anything other than their own bare hands. Hopefully it wouldn't happen on my watch.

The chaos quickly took a toll on my desire to stay sober, and I lapsed back into old habits to keep my sanity. Lavern and I were partying again. She and I had repaired our friendship after I escaped Ron's clutches and as my friend she understood and forgave me. She and I always had a good time together, and I was in desperate need of some fun in my life. She was integral in helping me to heal at that time; she taught me that even though we go through some shit in this life—and there will always be shit—it's never too much to stop the laughter and fun. However, she was not aware of the extent of *my* shit. Life picked up where I'd left it a few months earlier. Once again I was angry and really didn't give a fuck.

We found a nightclub that we'd frequent two to three nights a week where we'd drink our faces off, dance our asses off, and laugh. Over time we became familiar and partied with the owners and staff there, so it seemed only natural for us to accept jobs working there in the coat check room. It wasn't a well-paying job, but I was unemployed and broke and confident I knew how to make good tips. My father had taught how to accentuate my attributes and being a sexy little cock tease had its perks. Our job was to take people's coats and some would tip us. I already knew that the less we wore, and the sexier we danced, the more tips and drinks we received.

This job wasn't like working; it was more like having my own little dance party in the coat cubicle because there was always a flurry of excited people by the front doors. I was making friends who were happy to be around me, and I received the attention I'd been conditioned to seek since birth. I was taught that this was my destined life and I was living it like there was no tomorrow.

I was skeptical the first time I was invited to a ladies' night that included male strippers but my new girlfriends assured me, "You will *love* it!"

I wasn't interested in men or sex or the lessons that were attached to either, but because there was alcohol involved I'd give it a whirl. Ironically enough, that's what I received in return because halfway through the show one of the dancers gyrated in front of me and literally stirred my drink for me—and not with his finger! I was disgusted and oddly amused by this as he offered to buy our table new drinks and the party moved on.

After that night, my girlfriends and I found a new ladies' night for every day of the week that ended in a Y. I was on a head-to-toe rollercoaster high that involved intoxication, laughter, loud bass, and more male strippers than you could shake a stick at.

I devoured the attention and compliments thrown at me and was more self-confident than ever before. Attractive men, who were desired by hordes of women, wanted to hang out with me, and it didn't take long for it to go straight to my head and straight to their beds.

Father knew best; I *was* a sexy little bitch.

I cared about myself as much as these men pretended to care about me. I found myself waking up in random beds and wondering how I got there. It didn't matter. I had been taught and learned well that I was good for one thing and the sexuality equation was inevitable.

Attention + sex = affection, and I was no longer starving.

One night I was out drinking and moving my body to the music, and when I looked to my right, there was a guy standing there staring at me. I glared back at him with a cocked brow and a *what the fuck are you looking at?* expression.

He introduced himself and offered me a drink, which I accepted. I downed the one I had to get my hand ready for another. He told me that he'd seen me around and that he had wanted to ask me out but was too shy. I was flattered but didn't really care what he was talking about; I wasn't looking for anything other than a full glass.

His next comment grabbed my full attention. "I love your work."

I wasn't sure what he meant because my current job was hanging coats in the same club we were standing in, and I didn't really consider that work.

He explained that he meant my work as a model, not a coat check girl. He explained that he worked in the photo lab where my photographer developed my pictures. He leered at me hungrily and told me he really liked what he saw. He told me that my photographer looked a little sketchy, but I had a really hot body and he wouldn't mind rubbing it against his.

Apparently his liquid courage was working overtime.

I was shocked by his revelation and corrected him. "That's not my photographer; that's my father."

Then the gravity of that statement dawned on me. I'd just completely mortified myself and needed to escape. I turned and tried to walk away as he groped at my breast and laughed at me.

I pushed his hand off and bolted into the ladies' room and shut myself in a stall where I tried to compose myself. I heard the bathroom door open and someone walk in. A moment later the stall door was shoved open and he lunged at me.

"I think you're hot. Show me yours, and I'll show you mine."

He manipulated my breast in his grip again and pushed me up against the wall behind the toilet. This was one time I was thankful that I'd had to fight so much in my life and that I possessed so much pent up anger. I punched him repeatedly in his face and chest, and was able to throw him off balance. I pushed him out of the way and fled the bathroom. I was mad and didn't allow being manhandled in life, and definitely not by this piece of shit that thought he knew me.

Visibly disheveled and distressed, I ran to find one of the bouncers. I told him that some guy had just tried to fuck with me in bathroom. He called for backup from the other bouncers and asked me to show him the guy, and told me that he would take care of it. He was sitting across the bar laughing it up with his buddies as if nothing had happened. I was filled with so much rage in that instant that I couldn't control myself. I ran over to where he was, grabbed a barstool from behind him and swung it at his head with every ounce of my body. Within seconds there were three bouncers on him who dragged his kicking and flailing ass from the bar. I thought I needed the protection of a man, but I had protected myself and didn't need anyone to do that for me.

A new bouncer that I didn't really know came to check on me and ask what happened. I was embarrassed and only mentioned the attack portion. I didn't know this guy, and I wasn't going to spill my guts to him. I knew his name was Steve. He and I only talked briefly, but I could tell that he and I were entirely different people. He was shy and quiet, me not so much. He didn't drink, smoke cigarettes or pot. I frequented them all, regularly.

We engaged in casual conversations after the fight incident, not in a flirtatious manner but one I wasn't accustomed to: friendly and unassuming. I learned that he and his siblings had been raised in the same house all their life by his two loving parents.

I did not.

To the naked eye it appeared that we had nothing in common, but I soon found out that was irrelevant because the thread that bound us was hope. We shared the same need for basic human companionship and were both in search of our own version of a blue sky. The only difference was that he had a plan in motion to achieve that. I wanted to learn more.

His personality was so easy-going and refreshing that I found myself relaxing around his calm presence. He wasn't trying to get into my pants and didn't seem to have a hidden agenda between my legs so over time we talked about more personal things in our lives. I began to trust him, and we became more involved with each other, which was nice. Different from what I was used to, but nice. It had been a long time since I'd met a man I trusted and didn't abuse me or want something from me.

I wanted to feel love in my life and quickly developed feelings for him, hoping he would feel the same.

He did not.

He was terrified by the idea of me, and rightfully so, because I was clearly a complete train wreck, with a caboose that contained my family on a track that was missing ties. He reassured me that it wasn't me and emotionally shared his reasons for searching for a blue sky of his own.

He explained that his long-time girlfriend had just broken up with him, he still loved her, and wasn't sure how he was going to move on. I sympathized with him. I knew how it felt to be alone and lonely.

Having him show me his weakness gave me the strength to be vulnerable to him and share the events of the last month. In a jumble of words, I divulged the soap opera that was my life. I told him about Ron, my recent nervous breakdown, my father's love for the landlady who was two years older than Ryan, him leaving my mother for her, and that some stranger had just pointed out to me how thoroughly disgusting of a man my father truly was. I melted into a pool of tears. It wasn't easy to tell him these things but afterward I felt like a shaken bottle of pop that's been opened and released its fizz into the world.

Our friendship was solidified after this conversation because he didn't run for the hills like I expected him to. Instead he included me in his plans for freedom. He told me that I could join him but that there were some stipulations I had to follow before he left in a couple of months' time.

No smoking of anything + no drinking = freedom.

He told me that he was working at the bar for extra money so he could take a trip on his motorcycle to clear his head. I was working at the bar so that I could make money to drink all the time and numb mine, but I liked his plan better. I quit drinking alcohol and smoking pot effective immediately but wasn't ready to give up cigarettes quite yet. Sobriety, here I come? It was hard to imagine.

He drove an FJ1200 Yamaha crotch rocket motorcycle, which I thought was pretty cool. I was raised on the back of a bike, but this was the first time it wasn't a Harley between my legs, and I liked it. My father was disgusted by this fact, but I didn't really care what he thought about anything at that point.

Itty Bitty Pieces and the Great Escape

Combat on the home front had calmed down for the most part as my father was in the process of moving in with his new family and my mother was responsibly taking care of Paul. I was spending less time at my house and more time with Steve and his family, where I was able to witness how a typical family behaved.

It was nothing like I'd experienced at my house. Purple skies were still roiling but the prospect of leaving for potential clear skies was becoming more of a reality as I spent time with his family. There was joyous laughter, a general happiness, acceptance, and warmth in their home that wasn't in mine, and it soothed my frazzled nerves to be near these qualities.

I was eagerly saving up for the trip and was making payments on a protective leather suit, helmet, and boots that matched Steve's and the bike. We planned to leave in six months.

I trusted Steve and felt safe in confiding events to him that I'd never uttered to anyone with two legs and especially not a male. I told him about the pictures and the whole story about the guy in the bar and how confused I was. Was it not normal for a father to take pictures of his daughter like that while encouraging her to be a model? Was it not typical for him to have a poster-sized photo pasted on the wall of his daughter wearing nothing but a nude colored bra, panty, and garter belt set? A wall dedicated to photographs of his daughter in compromising positions for all to see? Or have hundreds of rolls, amounting to thousands of pictures, of his daughter and friends in less clothing than was required? My perception was clouded; up was down, and left was right.

I showed him a couple of the pictures, and the look on his face said it all. These were not normal photographs. He didn't offer me a verbal opinion, but suggested that I speak to his mom Ruth about it because she was a nurse and would know better.

I'd been living under torrential storm clouds for so long and had just identified that it was indeed a shit storm, but I needed validation that my thoughts were right.

I was scared to show his mom. I knew what she was going to say, and I was afraid that my very presence would disgust her as the pictures now did me. My eyes were wide open and for the first time I saw them for what they truly were, not what they were proposed to be, and I was not happy with the view.

I'd spent my life examining and studying people while staying unseen and silent. I didn't need to glimpse the split second flash of horror in her eyes as she blanched at the pictures to know her opinion. They weren't pictures taken by an adoring father of his young daughter but the product of a twisted and perverted obsession of a dirty old man. I was so pissed off at myself for not seeing it or recognizing it sooner, but I assure you that I was exponentially more pissed off at my father for doing it and my mother for allowing it happen right under her nose.

I stayed with his family that night. They alternately comforted me or left me in solitude though the emotional breakthrough I was experiencing. The one thing that I thought was a reality in my life, the love of my father, the only parent I ever felt love or affection from was an illusion. I was a puppet in his games of dress-up and *do as you're told*, and I was torn between how sad I was at a lost childhood for both myself and Paul and how much I despised him for brainwashing me into thinking it was okay to treat me that way. I was his child. Who could do that to their own child?

The next day I courageously phoned my father and made arrangements to meet him at his new girlfriend's condo. He was now living with her and her children.

I felt weak but sounded strong as I told him, "I need to talk to you right away about something important."

The thought of this confrontation terrified me because I'd seen his temper and knew that no one crossed him. If anyone attempted to go up against him, he'd knock them down to size, quick, quick!

Through immeasurable tears and the genuine nurturing I'd received the night before, I felt a small spark of love for myself. This was a foreign feeling to me but allowed me to think clearly about the situation at hand, and I had something to say about it, right now.

I boldly marched up and rang the bell. He opened the door and attempted to hug me in greeting. I brushed past him not wanting him to touch me. I thought: *Please don't let him touch me.* It was bad enough that I had to look deep into his mean brown eyes to make sure that I stayed strong. They now reminded me of the first man who'd sexually assaulted me at the auction when I was eight. I wasn't scared though. I'd been taught well in the tactics of intimidation by the best, and he was about to get a dose of his own teachings.

I stood in front of him with new-found confidence and adrenaline coursing through my veins. I was fired up but hoped I appeared calm. I mustered up my courage and said, "Collect all of the pictures and negatives that you have of me."

He crossed his arms over his chest and stood his ground as he examined my eyes for a moment and analyzed my glare. I stared back aggressively. At first I thought he was going to put up a fight but was pleasantly surprised when he didn't.

He threw his hands into the air, said okay, and walked away from me to collect what I'd requested. I sat there for what seemed like an eternity feeling a heightened sense of numbness as I maintained my coldness towards the man that I'd once called daddy.

Before leaving my house I'd grabbed a pair of sharp scissors and placed them in my purse. My plan was to destroy the one thing that he had let destroy me. Those pictures and that man had taken away my blue-skied wheat field, and I was about to take away something that made his sky blue—me.

When he returned he handed me a large number of pictures. I knew it wasn't nearly all of them; he would never give them all up. I wondered if he'd retrieved them from the white suitcase or his trunk of secrets. I scanned stacks of my life in various poses and outfits that he placed me in over the years, my revulsion growing with every flip.

I achieved a feeling of great satisfaction with every snip-snip of the scissors. I cut up almost every photo and negative that he'd given me, leaving a large pile of refuse on the floor that represented how he'd made me feel about myself up to that point. A few I kept and placed in my purse as a reminder of his perversions. It did not dawn on me at the time that I was also destroying evidence; I was just taking it away from him, which was all that mattered. He sat and watched me, slowly rocking in his chair, but I never looked at him for a second longer than I had to.

When I was satisfied I'd caused enough destruction, I picked myself off the floor and brushed myself free of the filth I was surrounded by.

I made my way towards the door but before leaving I turned back around to face him. When our eyes met again I knew that something had changed in us both, and it brought a joyous grin to my face because I had defeated him and was strong while he looked weak and pathetic.

I calmly said, "I think you're a disgusting human being and those pictures were as sick as you are."

I told him that I'd never be his subject again and that he should never try to contact me. I was so done with his bullshit, lies and purple sky illusions. I decided from that moment on that he would never darken my world again because I'd seen the light, and I was moving hopefully and purposefully in its direction.

Just as I opened the door to make my final escape from his lecherous and manipulative control his girlfriend walked in. I scowled at her like she was a stain on my favorite sweater and she looked back like I was a bug on her new shoe; neither of us were happy.

I seized the opportunity to give her a brief reality check; like the pile on the floor wasn't enough. She was a woman and a mother who appeared to care for her children. Surely she wanted to protect them from harm. I barely knew them, but my mother bear instincts hoped she would listen to me if I warned her to save her young children from the clutches of the monster she was living with.

I was wrong.

Instead of listening, she pushed me aside. "You're a liar just like your mother."

Her words were like a physical slap. I was nothing like my mother! My words had fallen on deaf ears and my heart broke for her children as I walked away. My only hope was that she'd realize her mistake quickly, and they would be safe from the blue sky stealing demon.

I left and didn't look back.

A few days later I went with Steve to make the final payment on my leather suit as we continued our plans to escape our realities. I felt anxious about leaving that day because my father was coming over to get the rest of his belongings, and I'd vowed never to see him again.

My mother promised me that it would be fine, and they wouldn't fight in front of Paul, but I didn't believe it. Her word meant absolutely nothing to me, but I grudgingly left him there hoping they were responsible enough to curb their anger for a bit.

When I returned home the first sound I heard was Paul repeatedly screaming at the top of his lungs. It sounded like someone was being murdered inside our condo. I thought: *Please don't let them have found where I stashed the gun!*

I tried not to panic as we ran through the door and up the stairs. Steve was gob-smacked into a temporary state of shock, and all I thought about was how to keep my head for Paul's sake.

I scanned the area to assess the damage. There was blood smeared on the bathroom door and my mother was in the bathroom screaming and ranting hysterically. I peered inside to see her smashing her head against the side of the bathtub, blood splattering on her face. My father was standing on the opposite side of the room huffing and puffing and gripping a rope murderously in his white-knuckled hands. He had a scratch on his face and looked at me like I'd just ruined his master plan. If looks could kill, I would've been dead.

In the middle of all of this chaos sat an innocent young boy wailing in distress. He was rocking back and forth with his hands over his ears screaming, "No!"

How was that not enough to make them stop?

I gathered my bleating cub into my arms and reassured him I was there, and that he was safe. I told him to go with Steve who I instructed to take him outside to his vehicle and play the radio loudly. Glaring at my father, I grabbed the phone and aggressively dialed 911 to come and assist my mother. My father dropped his rope and quickly left while I waited for help to arrive.

Although I didn't have a relationship with my mother I knew that I needed to get her and Paul the hell out of there. She'd given me life; it was the least I could do for her.

As much as I would've loved to keep Paul safe myself, I knew that I couldn't. I was leaving in a short time, and there was no way I was cancelling that because my parents couldn't act like adults. I would have to find a way to persuade my mother to be a parent and possibly get some help for herself, so that I could help myself.

I spoke with Ruth, Steve's mom, and she suggested that I call a local battered women's shelter to keep both of them safe and out of harm's way.

Once again I was forced to make a selfish decision that involved leaving Paul for the sake of my own sanity. Although my mother was a flake, she did love Paul and was never as mean to him as she was with me. I harbored hope that with me and my father completely gone she'd be able to get her life in order. I made a few phone calls and was able to arrange for us to stay at a shelter that very night. I stayed with them for the first couple of nights because there was no way that I was leaving that little boy's side, but I was an adult, and I was not battered. Not on the outside anyways.

I left after that. I needed my mother to take some responsibility and be a parent to Paul. As odd as it may sound, although I didn't like my mother or anything she stood for, which was nothing, I still had love for her. My heart went out to her, and I felt compelled to help her. I hoped she'd take this opportunity to get her life in order, not only for this innocent child, but for herself now that she was away from the devil himself.

With the permission of Steve's parents, I was able to stay with them until I could figure out other living arrangements, which was about a week later.

Through the shelter, my mother was able to find a house to rent for her and Paul. She was seeing a psychologist and seemed present of mind. I wanted to spend some time with them before I left, so I stayed there too. I could only hope that my mother was going to keep away from my father.

My mother was still in contact with Ryan who for the most part remained uninvolved. He was twenty-three, divorced, and battling his own addictions and demons. She'd lent him some money a few days previous, and he'd come over to the house earlier in the day and paid it back.

Later that night he returned to the house intoxicated and asked our mother for some of the money back. He needed it and said he'd replace it the next day.

I quickly told Paul, "Go listen to music in your room and to stay there until I come to get you."

He knew by now to listen to me.

My mother knew how Ryan operated when it came to paying back his debts: tomorrow never comes. When she said no I could feel the energy shift in the house from toxic to radioactive in the course of one small word.

His switch had been tripped and he went from talking calmly to flipping-the-fuck-out. He screamed at her and attempted to grab her purse that was on the floor beside her. She blocked his advances, using her body as a shield. She was no match against his strength, but she defended herself, and I was proud of her for that for half a split second until I had to react.

I wasn't scared, and I wasn't gonna tolerate this shit.

My world moved at the speed of light while my mind was stuck in slow motion as I grabbed for the phone to dial 911. He noticed what I was doing and reared back in my direction to stop the call. He knew if the police showed up he was going back to jail, and he most definitely didn't want that.

Ryan snatched the base of the phone and smacked me across the face with it, leaving me dazed with a black eye, and ran out the door. While we waited for the police I was furious with my mother for putting Paul in another violent and preventable situation. I made sure that I verbally smacked some sense into her head. I was so sick of fighting.

Cliff Notes version of my ranting: She was her own responsibility. Paul needed protecting and was her responsibility. Ryan needed to go back to jail, also her responsibility. And I was no longer involved, my choice and my responsibility.

When the police arrived I was proud of her for pressing charges against my brother and a restraining order was issued, which satisfied me that he wouldn't be around while I was gone. I stayed with Paul that night, and we sang and hummed until he fell asleep knowing that he was safe and loved.

A few weeks later Steve and I embarked on an adventure promising clear blue skies that signified so many things that weren't visible on the surface.

My life in a nutshell: I was drinking regularly, smoking cigarettes and marijuana since the age of ten. I was sexually assaulted five times by four different men by the time I was sixteen years old, two of which were incestuous. I was taught that I was a disposable, unlovable object that didn't matter. I was manipulated to believe this was acceptable. This was further validated by a violent relationship and harsh realizations about the people who were my family. I'd moved eighteen times and was a *Purple Sky Survivalist ~ Growing Up a Victim of Illusions* and I was soon going to be free.

Free of being Paul's pseudo mother. Free of my mother's and brother's violence and explosive tempers. Free from my father's forever lingering stare and grasp. And I was completely free of intoxicants in a decade.

During tearful good-byes that I shared with both Paul and oddly enough my mother, she assured me that she'd keep him safe while I was away. I guaranteed her that I'd be checking in. It was the first selfless act that I'd seen from her in my direction and it gave me hope that I'd finally reached her. Paul deserved a life that matched his sparkling blue eyes and didn't include the things that he'd already witnessed.

On September 1, 1988, at 11:07 am, Steve and I watched Alberta disappear in the rearview mirrors. Anticipation, apprehension and anxiety zipped through my veins as we flew down the highway. We were on an uncharted adventure of self-healing, self-realization and sobriety for an undetermined amount of time.

I was 20 years old.

Photographs

Age15: Following orders as my father instructed me to "lick my lips and open my mouth." He designed, cut and sewed this dress for me for Billy Barker Days in Quesnel, B.C.

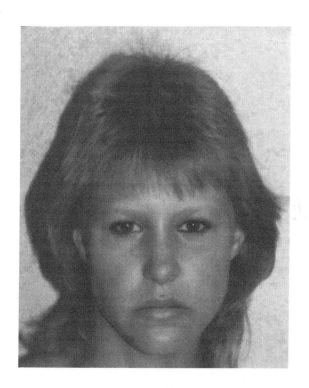

Age 16: This is the face of an innocent girl who survived under purple skies. Can sense the sadness in her eyes?

Age18: My typical look displaying my lack of self-worth

Age19: Posing before work. Notice the shrine of photographs of me on the wall. Normal, right?

Age 19: This wicker chair was one of my father's favorite props and I'm wearing clothing from his trunk of secrets.

This is one of the last pictures that he ever took of me.

Gratitude!

Honestly, words cannot express the genuine and eternal gratefulness I feel for my tribe of loving and supportive blue sky family and friends. Without a doubt, if not for you I would not be here to share my story and help others to heal from theirs. Thank you for continuing to join hearts and hands with me on this journey we call life.

I love you!

A warm and sincere shout out of gratitude to my professional team of powerhouse business women, authors and new-found friends who have generously helped me to reveal the heart beneath the hurt through this series of books. Thank you!

Purple Sky Survivalist was truly built by a village.

I am proud, blessed and thankful each and every day that I'm alive and thriving and able to fulfill my passions in life. As a writer, public speaker and survivor of incest, abuse and addiction I can only hope that I've created a book you will find worthy of your time. May you find some healing within yourself through my journey and be inspired to explore what makes your heart happy and your sky blue.

I should have been a statistic but I'm not. Neither are you. You are reading my words and you are not alone.

What is your next step in *your* journey?

To book Deborah to speak at your next event:

deborahkinisky.com or purpleskysurvivalist.com

Email: blueskythrivalist@gmail.com

To follow on social media:

facebook.com/Deborah-Kinisky-137085510049641

facebook.com/groups/DeborahKiniskyHerStoryVictimToVictorious

facebook.com/SurvivalistToThrivalist

Instagram: deborah.kinisky

Twitter, LinkedIn, Pinterest: deborahkinisky

Please watch for the adventures I experienced on my road to freedom in my next book, Survivalist to Thrivalist! Coming soon!

I look forward to sharing with you and hearing from you!

Wishing you clear blue skies.

Deborah

Made in the USA
Charleston, SC
13 February 2017